LIVERPOOL
JOHN MOORES UNIVERSITY
I.M. MARSH LIBRARY
BARKHILL ROAD
LIVERPOOL L17 6BD
TEL. 0151 231 5216/5299

PRO Readers' Guide No 18

WITHDRAWN

Education

Books are to be returned on or before
the last date below.

2 5 APR 2005

- 9 FEB 2006

7-DAY LOAN

D1477347

I.M. MARSH LIBRARY LIVERPOOL L17 6BD
TEL. 0151 231 5216/5299

PRO Publications

LIVERPOOL JMU LIBRARY

3 1111 00748 9436

Acknowledgements

I would like to thank Dr Paul Sharp of the School of Education, University of Leeds and Professor W B Stephens for their invaluable comments on early drafts of this Readers' Guide; and Amanda Bevan, Anne Howers and Ysanne Stiel-McNeil for their help and advice. Sarah Price deserves special mention for her help with the final text. I am also very grateful to Roger Nixon for allowing me to use items belonging to his great aunt Maud Elliott in this Guide.

PRO Publications
Kew
Richmond
Surrey TW9 4DU

Crown Copyright 1997
ISBN 1 873 162 33 2

A catalogue card for this book
is available from the British Library

CONTENTS

LIST OF ILLUSTRATIONS

1.   INTRODUCTION

The purpose of this readers' guide is to help researchers find their way through the records of the various education departments held by the Public Record Office (PRO). It is intended as much for the student of the history of education as for the pupil seeking information relating to his or her own school. It seeks to explain, in simple terms, how the education records fit together, to offer some guidance on what they contain and to make some suggestions on how they may be used.

It may be helpful to remember that, broadly speaking, many records of the education departments can be divided into the following five main categories: general policy files, institution files, local education authority files, endowment files and inspectorate papers. You should also note that the terms 'elementary' and 'secondary' are not wholly suitable when applied to nineteenth century schools. Grammar schools, for instance, often provided elementary instruction as well as 'grammar'. Private schools for the middle classes and even some charity schools provided both elementary and more advanced instruction.

1.1   Content of Records

The records of the education departments were created for the administrative use of central government departments and continue to be arranged and catalogued not by subject but by the way in which they were originally used, ie by their administrative function. While it is possible, for example, to find information on individual schools it is scattered throughout a number of different classes. To help you track down material relating to a particular school, case studies for elementary (primary) and secondary schools have been included in this guide. You should note that, although references sometimes occur to named teachers, eg in Preliminary Statements (ED 7) or occasionally in early HMI reports (ED 17), it is not possible to trace the career of an individual teacher through the records of the education departments. Similarly, although some records sometimes contain the names of pupils, eg Endowed School Files (ED 27), this is rare. Census returns (not covered in this guide) do contain the names of both teachers and pupils at boarding schools on the day the census was taken.

You are likely to find detailed information about individual schools, teachers and pupils at the appropriate local record office. These records will include log books, admission registers, punishment books, plans, school prospectuses, inspectors' reports, governors' minutes, accounts, staff registers, teachers' association minutes, examination schedules, etc (*see 1.5 Useful Addresses*).

1.2   PRO References

Each volume or file in the Public Record Office has an identifying number. To order a record you have to know its number. Most reference numbers consist of three parts: letter code, class number and piece number.

Reference number component	Explanation
letter code	shows the government department which created the record eg **ED** = education departments
class numbers	show the type of record eg **109** = Reports on Secondary Institutions
piece numbers	identify the particular file eg **126** = inspector's report for Kendrick Girls' School, 1903

Piece numbers are given in the left hand margin of the class list with a date and description of each piece on the right. In some class lists the original file reference assigned by the department which created the file is given on the right hand margin.

The lists (catalogues) of some of the classes referred to in this guide are arranged by subject rather than in strict numerical order. To use these classes effectively, you should refer to the list of subject codes given at the beginning of the class list.

eg   ED 24 Private Office Papers 1851-1935

SUBJECT	CODE
Adult Education	1
Agriculture	2
Anson papers	3
Art	4
General	4/1
Royal College of Art	4/2
School of Art	4/3
Associations	5
Attendance	6

Bills	7
Board of Education Bill, 1899	7/1
Canal Boats Bill 1929	7/2
Children (Employment and School Attendance) Bill 1914	7/3

Classes arranged in this way also contain a key to cross references from the piece numbers to the relevant code number.

1.3   Legislation Index

This is an index to records in the PRO dealing with the preparation, administration, interpretation and subsequent amendment of post-1900 Acts of Parliament. It contains an entry for each Act of Parliament (or Bill) for which relevant records have been identified. Most entries refer to individual pieces in a class, but where a large number of pieces in a class (more than ten) refer to the Act, only the class code and title (or a brief description) are cited. Records subject to extended closure are not included in the Legislation Index.

There is a separate entry for each Act, arranged in chronological order (the year in which the Act was passed) and by chapter number. At the top right-hand corner of each page are four digits divided by a full stop (eg 44.31). The first two digits represent the calendar year, and the next two represent the chapter number of the act (therefore 44.31 is the 31st act passed in the year 1944, ie Education Act 1944).

Within each Act the entries are arranged alphabetically by the name of the department with the main responsibility for creating the record. Within each creating department (eg Board of Education) the entries are arranged by document reference, ie alphabetically by lettercode and then numerically by class number and piece number.

1.4   Parliamentary Papers

The House of Commons Parliamentary Papers are available in the PRO on microfiche. They are arranged by microfiche filing number, which relates to each individual microfiche containing a particular year and volume. References to Parliamentary Papers in this guide take the form

House	year	volume number
HC	1861	xxi

To identify precisely where a particular item is in a volume, you can either look at the contents list on the first microfiche for the volume or use the CD-ROM index available in the Microfilm Reading Room (MRR). The example cited will produce the report of the Newcastle Commission on elementary education, 1861. The cabinets in the MRR are labelled with the years, volume numbers and microfiche filing numbers of the items they contain. A self-service system operates in the MRR.

1.5   Useful Addresses

Addresses of local authority and other record offices mentioned in this guide will be found in *British Archives (3rd edition)*, ed Janet Foster and Julia Shepherd (Basingstoke, 1995).

Examples:

British and Foreign School Society Archives Centre
　　　Brunel University College
　　　Lancaster House
　　　Borough Road
　　　Isleworth
　　　Middx TW9 5DU
Access Policy: Generally open to public, no prior appointment necessary.

The Church of England Record Centre
　　　15 Galleywall Road
　　　Bermondsey
　　　London SE16 3PB
Incorporates records/former archives of National Society for Promoting Religious Education
Access Policy: Bona fide researchers, by appointment. Records open to public (100 year closure on personal files, 30 year closure on certain administrative files.)

Charity Commission for England and Wales
　　　St Alban's House
　　　57/60 Haymarket
　　　London
　　　SW1Y 4QX
Access Policy: Central Register of Charities is open to the public, charity records over 30 years old are open to inspection on application.

The Department for Education and Employment Information Bureau (formerly the Department of Education and Science Library), Sanctuary Buildings, Great Smith Street, London SW1 3BT, encourages enquirers to approach the Institute of Education Library, University of London, the British Library or their own local reference library initially and permits access to its holdings in limited circumstances when a publication cannot be located elsewhere.

2.   ADMINISTRATIVE HISTORY

In a half empty House of Commons in August 1833 Lord Althorp proposed

> That a sum, not exceeding twenty thousand pounds, be granted to
> His Majesty, to be issued in aid of Private Subscriptions for the
> Erection of School Houses, for the Education of the Children of
> the Poorer Classes in Great Britain.

The suggestion was accepted by a vote of 50 in favour against 26. Direct financial involvement in education had begun.

The Treasury administered the grant. To receive it, support from one of the voluntary education bodies, like the National Society for the Education of the Poor in the Principles of the Established Church or the British and Foreign School Society, was essential. Preference was given to applications from large towns and cities. It was an interim measure.

2.1   Committee of the Privy Council on Education, 1833-1899

Demand for popular education increased but attempts to satisfy it were bedevilled by religious controversy between Anglicans and Nonconformists, effectively jeopardizing the passage of any education bill through Parliament. To circumvent this Lord John Russell advised the Queen to use the Royal Prerogative to create a special department of the Privy Council to supervise these parliamentary grants. Thus by an Order in Council of April 1839 the Committee of the Privy Council on Education (PCCE) was born (PC 2/221). It was to consist of not more than five members: the President of the Council, the Lord Privy Seal, the Chancellor of the Exchequer, the Home Secretary and the Master of the Mint.

The first secretary to this committee was Dr James Kay-Shuttleworth, a man with first-hand experience of the working conditions of the poor and a conviction that education was the key to their improvement. The three main tasks of the committee were to help in the establishment of schools, to provide funds towards the training of teachers and to inspect the grant-aided schools.

2.2   Education Department, 1856-1899

The *Report on the Organization of the Permanent Civil Service* (known as the Northcote-Trevelyan Report), which was produced in 1853 (HC 1854 xxvii), recommended that the Education Committee be separated from the Privy Council Office. This was achieved by an Order in Council of 25 February 1856 (PC 2/243). A new Education Department was created which incorporated the Science and Art

Department of the Board of Trade. In theory the general educational work of the new department was controlled by the PCCE but in practice the Department operated as a virtually autonomous unit. Similarly the Science and Art Department, although nominally part of the Education Department, continued to function as a separate entity (*see 5.1*).

The survival rate of records of the PCCE and the Department of Education has not been high. The introductory note to the aptly named Miscellanea (ED 9) explains why as follows:

> A few files and volumes appear to have escaped by chance the severe and general destruction of certain classes of records of the nineteenth century. A collection thus arises of Minute Books, correspondence, reports etc neither large nor complete, which defy classification, yet contribute to the study of educational history.

Only one manuscript volume of the minutes of the PCCE for the years 1839 to 1841 has survived (ED 9/1), together with the secretaries' minute books 1848 to 1871 and 1889 to 1900 (ED 9/4 and 5). One volume of typed copies of selected letters from old letter books for the period 1847-1858 exists (ED 9/12). There is also some correspondence about the election of members of school boards (ED 9/22).

ED 17 contains a set of printed minutes and reports of the PCCE which were published as command papers. Some correspondence of the Education Department with individual school boards will be found on the Parish Files (ED 2). Surviving correspondence of the presidents and vice-presidents is in ED 24. The Establishment Files (ED 23) include little material on the formation of the Education Department but there is a complete record from 1851 of correspondence between the department and the Treasury.

The Treasury Board Papers (T 1) form a major source of contemporary information about the work of the Education Department because very few files created by that department survive. Incoming documents to the Treasury were numbered sequentially from the beginning of each year so that, for example, 4978/39 refers to the document, or file, numbered 4978 in 1839. They were registered in numerical sequence, by correspondent alphabetically, and by department alphabetically, in the registers which now form the class T 2. In a typical year in the mid-nineteenth century some 25,000 documents were registered. As time went on some files were destroyed, and others were assembled by subject. A record of this process was maintained in the skeleton registers which now form the class T 3. Separate subject registers were begun in 1852 (T 108). The Treasury papers have been weeded (selectively destroyed). Mistakes were inevitably made in these processes and some files are unaccountably missing, either destroyed but not recorded as such, or removed from the system because of their importance, never returned and consequently lost.

In the early years after the formation of the PCCE the situation is confused because the Treasury was still dealing with many schools itself. In 1840, for example, more than 200 Treasury files were registered under 'Schools', the heading which included all Education Department business. By 1842 the number had dropped to less than sixty. After 1847, with the expansion and increasing complication of Education Department business, it rose again to over one hundred.

Most of the schools documents for the early years seem to be missing. They were probably the 'schools papers' recorded as requested from the Treasury by Kay-Shuttleworth in 1844 (24548/44 in T 1/5017/24657, 17 Dec 1844) which cannot be traced. A systematic search has been made among the Treasury Registers (T 2 and T 3) and Board Papers (T 1) for documents relating to education for the period 1839-1860 under the headings 'Schools' and 'Council Office' and the following papers were found concerning administration and organization:

1839	T 1/3405/28368	Miscellaneous
1840	T 1/4505/23036	Miscellaneous
1841	T 1/4566/4821	Kay's salary
1842	T 1/4676/1403	Payment to Thurgar
	4708/1176	Payment to Thurgar
	4728/17211	Durham memorial
1843	T 1/4900/26448	Miscellaneous
1844	T 1/4968/17384	Inquiry expenses
	5017/24657	Miscellaneous
1845	T 1/5086/19010	Libel action
	5086/19016	Small grants through the Post Office
1847	T 1/5238/1757	Payment for Dr Taylor
1848	T 1/5387/18307	Emigration scheme
	5391/19684	Franking letters
	5394/20112	Gratuity to Rapley
	5405/23431	Post Office money orders
	5413/24770	Increase for Lingen
1849	T 1/5479/15674	Staff reorganization
	5511/24917	Money orders

1850	T 1/5552/6372	Estimate for 1850-1851
	5591/20866	Money orders
	5609/24224	Promotions etc
	5656/5388	Legal business
1851	T 1/5676A/19035	Irish schoolbooks
	5701A/24566	Money orders
	5714B/25684	Establishment etc
1852	T 1/5737A/12919	Establishment etc
1853	T 1/5817B/19319	Irish schoolbooks
	5842A/24894	Committee of Inquiry, and appointments (Northcote-Trevelyan Committee)
	5845A/25361	Northcote-Trevelyan Committee
1854	T 1/5875B/14045	Account
	5906B/26392	Staffing etc
1855	T 1/5963A/18866	Staffing etc
	6622B/8537	Black-edged paper
1856	T 1/5989A/5918	Examiners
	6031A/19438	Amalgamation of departments
	6046A/20715	Lennard's accounts
	6048A/20841	Salaries etc
1857	T 1/6062A/7530	Examiners
	6082A/15282	Staffing etc
	6099A/19314	Lennard's accounts
1858	T 1/6116A/4284	Boothby's retirement
	6119A/6069	Woolley's transfer
	6119A/6070	Cowie's salary
	6127A/11164	Ordnance Survey maps
	6128A/11536	Auditing of Education Department accounts
	6132A/13358	Printing of reports
	6133A/13673	Additional assistant clerk
	6151B/18764	Irish schoolbooks
	6160A/20130	Newcastle Commission
	6168A/21074	Chester's retirement
	6774B/3682	Issue procedure

1859 T 1/6177B/2529	Bayly increase
6191A/10922	Staffing etc
6198A/13604	Printing reports
6199B/14156	Hutchinson's retirement
6219A/18974	Newcastle Commission
6227B/19906	Printing
1860 T 1/6250A/9059	Assistant clerks
6275A/18814	Printing reports
6276C/19078	Irish education
6283A/20075	Salaries etc

For details about what information the Treasury papers contain about individual schools see chapter 3.3 Building Grants.

With the establishment of a national system of elementary education after the Education Act 1870, it became increasingly difficult to control everything from the centre. In 1887 the then secretary to the Education Department, Patrick Cumin, told the Cross Commission (assessing progress in elementary education since 1870, *see 3.5*) that:

> The tremendous detail of looking into every school in the country was too cumbrous. It was all very well when education was a small affair, but now that it has become national . . . the system was too complicated.

By the end of the nineteenth century there were several central authorities concerned with different types of school - the Science and Art Department (art schools and technical schools), the Charity Commission (endowed schools), the Board of Agriculture (agricultural education), the Home Office (reformatory and industrial schools), the Admiralty (naval education), the War Office (military education) and the Local Government Board (poor law schools). The complexity was reflected at the local level where school boards, attendance committees, boards of managers, secondary schools, county councils and county borough councils all had some unco-ordinated involvement in education. Reorganization was effected by legislation in two stages.

2.3　　Board of Education, 1899-1944

An act of 1899 established the Board of Education, which replaced the Education Department and the Science and Art Department and took on the educational functions of the Charity Commissioners and the Board of Agriculture. However, the confused web of local boards, committees and councils remained.

Robert Morant, assistant director of the office of Special Inquiries and Reports, wished to simplify the local structures and abolish the school boards. He realised that many of the larger school boards were in breach of the law by providing money for post-elementary education when only legally permitted to finance elementary education. He seized the opportunity offered by a dispute between the London School Board and the London Technical Education Committee about the provision of post-elementary education. Morant ensured that those prosecuting the school board were aware that aiding post-elementary education was illegal. Immediately T B Cockerton, the government auditor, saw the point and disallowed to the London School Board expenditure on science and art classes in higher grade schools and on evening continuation classes on the grounds that a school board was competent to provide only elementary education. He won and the judgment was upheld in the court of appeal (ED 14/25-26, 41, 102; ED 24/83, 136; MH 27/141-142).

The activities of Morant and the repercussions of the Cockerton Judgment drew attention to the anomalous position of many school boards providing post-elementary education under legislation sanctioning only elementary education. The situation was regularized by the Education Act 1902, which abolished school boards and created the local education authorities (LEAs), allowing them to provide 'education other than elementary'.

The Board was organized by Morant into three main branches: Elementary, Secondary and Technical; two special branches: Legal and Medical and Special Services; two general ones: Accountant General and Establishments; together with three others: Welsh Department, Office of Special Inquiries and Reports and the Inspectorate. Although its remit was extended by the Education Acts of 1902, 1918 (which made the provision of education to the age of fourteen compulsory) and of 1921, the organization of the Board remained basically unaltered during its existence.

Information about the records produced by the various branches of the Board will be found in subsequent chapters. Bill Papers are in ED 31 and precedent books used by the Board for interpreting legislation and codes are in ED 27. ED 10 contains records relating to general educational questions. Schemes submitted by local authorities under the 1918 and 1921 Acts are in ED 13, ED 120 and ED 75. A series of obsolete forms is in ED 8. Private Office Papers covering all aspects of education are in ED 24 and ED 136. Establishment files are in ED 23, and ED 141 contains a set of Establishment minutes and notices.

Material used for the preparation of the official history of education during the Second World War is in ED 138; this history was never published but the class includes a number of draft chapters.

2.4   Ministry of Education, 1944-1964

In 1944, under the Education Act, the Board was replaced by a minister. The department underwent fundamental reorganization with the formation of the Schools

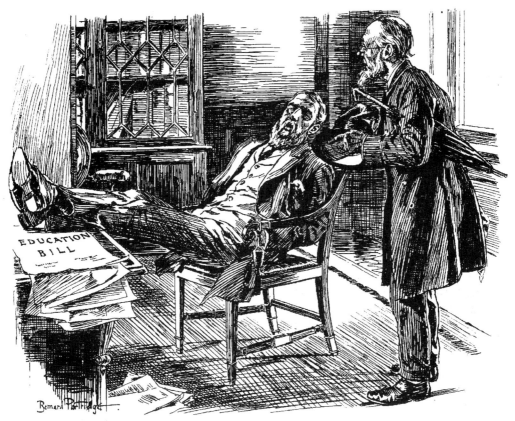

NOT WANTED!

Member of the School Board (*to the President of the Council*). "BUT UNDER THIS NEW EDUCATION BILL WHERE DO *I* COME IN?"
Duke of D-v-nshire. "AS FAR AS I REMEMBER, YOU *DON'T. YOU* GO OUT!"

Figure 1
'Not Wanted!' (*Punch*, April 16, 1902)

Branch and the Further Education Branch. The regional organization was also altered. The new ministry took over certain functions from other government departments: administration of the Camps Act 1939 from the Ministry of Health, the education of Polish refugees under the Polish Resettlement Act 1947, agricultural education from the Ministry of Agriculture, Fisheries and Food in 1959, and the remaining educational functions from the Charity Commissioners. The training of handicapped adults passed to the Ministry of Labour in 1945, the educational facilities at prisons and borstals went to the Prison Commission in 1953.

ED 142 contains the memoranda and circulars issued by the ministry. Private Office Papers, including files on post-war planning, are in ED 136; schemes for development plans for primary and secondary schools drawn up under the 1944 Act will be found in ED 151 and ED 152. Material relating to the education of Polish refugees is in ED 128. General education files are in ED 147 and ED 34 contains papers prepared to answer parliamentary questions, where they do not appear on the relevant registered file.

2.5   Department of Education and Science from 1964

The recommendations of the Trend Committee on the Civil Service (HC 1963-4 ix Cmnd 2171) and of the Robbins Committee on Higher Education (HC 1962-3 xi-xiv) led to the formation of the Department of Education and Science (DES) in April 1964. The new Department was created from the merger of the Ministry of Education and the Office of the Minister for Science. It also took on responsibility for the University Grants Committee.

During the 1970s the Welsh Office gradually took control of Welsh education: primary and secondary education came first in November 1970 and by 1978 only the universities were outside its remit. In 1971 the responsibility for the education of mentally handicapped children and for junior training centres was transferred to the DES from the Department of Health and Social Security.

Minutes, papers and surveys of the evidence taken by the Robbins Committee are in ED 116, ED 117 and ED 118 respectively.

3.   ELEMENTARY EDUCATION

3.1   State involvement in elementary education

State financial involvement in education began only in 1833. Earlier educational initiative was essentially private and very often religious. Elementary education was provided by dame schools or common day schools, both of which charged fees, and by charity schools, which were free.

3.2   Trust Deeds

Many trust deeds relate to school foundations. Between 1735 and 1925 the conveyance of land for charitable uses, expressly including school buildings and schoolmasters' houses after 1836, had to be enrolled on the Close Rolls of Chancery (C 54) until 1903 and thereafter in the Enrolment Books of the Supreme Court of Judicature (J 18). Supplementary trust deeds had to be enrolled if the school managers enlarged the site but not if they merely extended the buildings on an existing site. These enrolments often contain site plans. Further information about charitable trusts set up for educational purposes may be found at the Charity Commission (*see under Useful Addresses 1.5*).

There is an alphabetically arranged topographical index to trust deeds: to the end of 1870 in bound volumes and then to 1905 in card index form. After 1905 deeds can be traced only if the year of enrolment and the name of the donor or vendor are known. It is clear that a number of trust deeds, for which there is collateral evidence, escaped enrolment.

EXAMPLE:

Trust deed for Farnham National School: entry in topographical index:

Farnham co Surrey school at 1860.30.3

1860	=	year of enrolment
30	=	number or 'part' of Chancery roll for that year
3	=	entry number on roll

To find the correct Close Roll reference you need to key up the topographical index entry with the *List of Chancery Rolls* (Lists and Indexes XXVII, Kraus Reprint Corporation, 1963). The thirtieth part for 1860 is C 54/15454 and the third entry on that roll is the trust deed granting:

> Land adjoining the church yard, near West Street to the vicar of
> Farnham and successors . . . to be used for a school . . . conducted
> according to the principles of the National Society.

This became Farnham National School. The deed was signed and sealed on 21 February 1860 and enrolled on 19 March 1860.

Information about trust deeds will also be found among the Treasury Papers (T 1), eg 1849 T 1/ 5487/18018 and 1855 T 1/5980A/20562. These papers also contain the following files on endowments of Scottish schools:

1842	T 1/4553/16510	1844	T 1/5003/23748
	4688/5776	1845	5030/1352
	4763/23809		5061/13180

ED 191 contains the enrolled deeds for Church of England elementary schools made between 1903 and 1920 under the Mortmain and Charitable Trusts Acts 1888-1892 or the Technical and Industrial Institutions Act 1892. The class consists of four volumes of manuscript copies of the deeds on vellum. They contain seventy deeds with the name(s) of the grantor(s) and trustees, and the first managers. Each volume has an index at the front with the name and location of each school.

3.3   Building Grants

In August 1833 annual sums began to be voted by Parliament, for distribution by the Treasury, to supplement private money to build schools for poor children. From 1839 this grant-aid was made conditional on inspection (*see chapter 10*) and in England and Wales was distributed to voluntary bodies, such as the National Society or the British and Foreign School Society, for buildings or improvements. It continued until the provisions of the Elementary Education Act 1870 came into operation; no applications were accepted after 31 December that year. Some files of correspondence survive among the Treasury Board Papers on dealings of the PCCE with the National Society (1849 T 1/5473/13686; 1852 T 1/5741A/14620; 1853 T 1/5845A/25337).

Applications for aid are bound in volumes (ED 103) and relate to the grant, administered by the Treasury between 1833 and 1839 and subsequently by the PCCE, for the building of elementary schools. The applications, which cover schools in England, Wales and Scotland, are arranged neither alphabetically nor chronologically within the volumes. Access to them is provided by an index (ED 103/141), a copy of which is available in the Research Enquiries Room at Kew. The index is not straightforward to use. The significant numbers are in the columns marked 'Papers', subdivided into volume and page; it is the numbers or letters appearing here which

THE THREE R's; OR, BETTER LATE THAN NEVER.

RIGHT HON. W. E. FORSTER (CHAIRMAN OF BOARD). "WELL, MY LITTLE PEOPLE, WE HAVE BEEN GRAVELY AND EARNESTLY CONSIDERING WHETHER YOU MAY LEARN TO READ. I AM HAPPY TO TELL YOU THAT, SUBJECT TO A VARIETY OF RESTRICTIONS, CONSCIENCE CLAUSES, AND THE CONSENT OF YOUR VESTRIES — *YOU MAY!*"

Figure 2
'The Three R's, Or, Better Late Than Never (*Punch*, March 26, 1870)

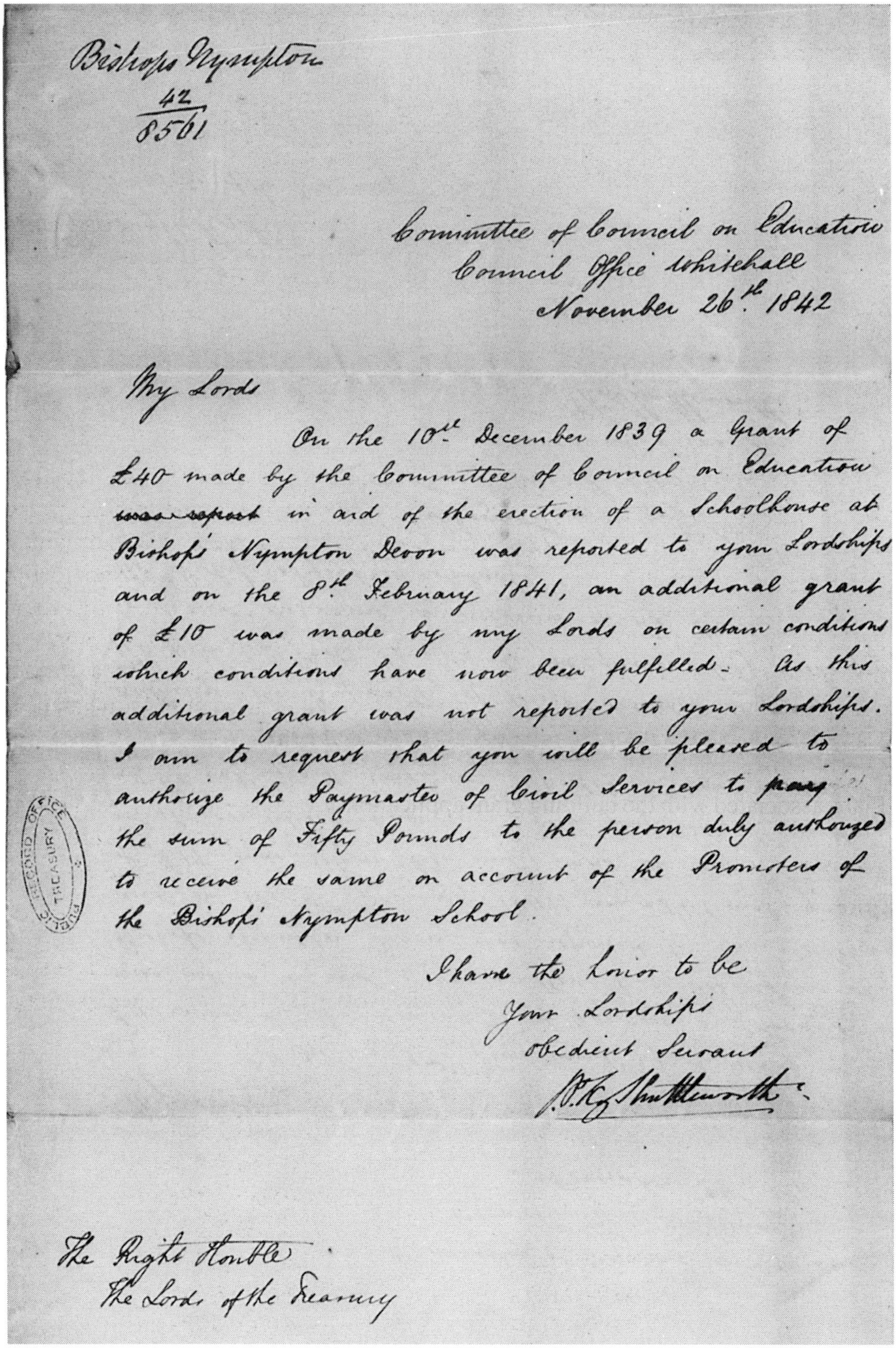

Bishops Nympton
42/8561

Committee of Council on Education
Council Office Whitehall
November 26th. 1842

My Lords

On the 10th. December 1839 a Grant of £40 made by the Committee of Council on Education ~~was repaid~~ in aid of the erection of a Schoolhouse at Bishops' Nympton Devon was reported to your Lordships and on the 8th February 1841, an additional grant of £10 was made by my Lords on certain conditions which conditions have now been fulfilled. As this additional grant was not reported to your Lordships. I am to request that you will be pleased to authorize the Paymaster of Civil Services to ~~pay~~ the sum of Fifty Pounds to the person duly authorized to receive the same on account of the Promoters of the Bishops' Nympton School.

I have the honor to be
Your Lordships
obedient Servant
J. K. Shuttleworth

The Right Honble
The Lords of the Treasury

PUBLIC RECORD OFFICE
TREASURY

Figure 3
Request for a grant of Treasury money to Bishop's Nympton School, Devon, 1842 (T 1/ 4779/25337)

should be keyed with the ED 103 list. There are, for example, the following two entries under Farnham, Surrey:

Place	Papers		Reference
	Vol	**Page**	
Farnham NS	77	453	ED 103/77 p 453
Farnham B	136	381	ED 103/136 p 381

NS	=	National Society	=	Church of England
B	=	British and Foreign School Society	=	Nondenominational

ED 103/77 pp 453-475   Farnham National School

These papers relate to the application for a building grant made in 1859 and received in 1860. They include information about the dimension of the planned buildings, the windows, roofs and the ventilation, together with details of the income and expenditure of the school. There are also eight pages listing contributions by ratepayers giving the name and address of each contributor, the annual value at which the property is assessed in the parish and the amount of the contribution. The committee of management of the school certifies that the work has been carried out; the architect also signs the certificate. A balance sheet of the building account of Farnham new National School is included showing the total cost as £2587 17s 4d.

Plans associated with the building grant applications are generally preserved in local record offices, but a small number of coloured plans contemporary with the grant applications have recently been transferred to the PRO (ED 228). *See chapter 12 for further details.*

Additional information about these grants may be found in the Treasury Papers (T 1), with registers in T 2 and T 3 (see 2.2). The following files, registered as 'grant business' have been identified for the period 1839-1860:

1842	T 1/4779/24337	1854	T 1/5861B/6172
1843	4894/25938		5894B/23195
1845	5089/19414	1857	6050B/1000
	5128/24913	1858	6129A/11981
1846	5140/1681		6133B/13916
	5150/6446		6133B/14069
	5198/21828		6153A/19126
	5209/24419	1859	6176B/1783
1847	5264/14126		6186A/8147
	5310/26809		6191A/10814
1848	5440/27682	1860	6254B/11440

1849	5445/2165	6255B/11786
	5465/10796	6278B/19339
	5529/27679	5529/27679

eg T 1/4779/25337 is a file of correspondence about grants for building schools in 1842 and covers applications from Scotland, England, Wales and Guernsey.

Data on building grants made for the years 1834-1837 is given in the annual Parliamentary Papers, Accounts of Sums granted in aid of Erection of Schools. The amount and date of award of grant for elementary schools appear in the appendixes to the Minutes and Reports of the Committee of the Privy Council on Education (ED 17), under the heading 'Schools aided by Parliamentary Grant'. These reports were published as Parliamentary Papers and that particular appendix became known after 1906 as List 21.

Before a school received a grant its promoters were required to submit a preliminary statement. This recorded details of the tenure and establishment of the school, its income and expenditure and information about accommodation and staffing. Surviving preliminary statements for elementary schools 1846-1924 are in ED 7 and after 1924 on the school files in ED 21. No preliminary statement survives for either of the Farnham examples cited above but there are later ones (ED 7/118) which are dealt with at 3.9.

3.4   Surveys and Reports

At the beginning of the nineteenth century a survey of school provision by parish was made for Parliament and printed as *The Abstract of the Answers and Returns Relative to the Poor* (HC 1803-4 xiii) which provided details of the state of parochial schools. A further survey was undertaken in 1816 by a select committee of the House of Commons under the chairmanship of H P (later Lord) Brougham; information was supplied by parish clergy. The results were published in the *Digest of Parochial Returns* (HC 1819 ix). They are arranged by county, provide details of the capacity of the endowed, unendowed and Sunday schools and distinguish between National, British and dame schools, but they do not give the names of individual schools (see Bebington example in case study at 3.14). T 74/3 includes some returns of elementary school provision in 1816. A similar survey was undertaken in 1833 and its results were published two years later as *Abstract of Education Returns* (HC 1835 xli-xliii).

An inquiry into education in England was conducted as part of the 1851 ecclesiastical census. A small number of the returns, which were voluntary, survives among Home Office records of the census (HO 129). One particularly comprehensive example of the returns is available for the registration district of Keighley (HO 129/494). It consists of one complete volume with returns for schools of all types - day, boarding,

494-1-1 ___13

31

$\mathfrak{Census}$ of $\mathfrak{Great}$ $\mathfrak{Britain}$, 1851.

RETURN of the several Particulars in accordance with the Act of 13 & 14 Vict., cap. 53, to be inquired into respecting the undermentioned

SCHOOL.

GENERAL INSTRUCTION.

This Return applies to all Schools whatever in which Daily Tuition is carried on, whether Public or Private, whether intended for the higher, the middle, or the lower classes; including, therefore, all Public Collegiate ...ls, Endowed Grammar Schools, Private Classical and Commercial Schools, Schools in connection with the ...nal or other School Society, Dame or Infant Schools, Ragged Schools, Workhouse Schools, Prison ...ls, &c. &c.

The Return is to be filled up by the Master, Mistress, or other principal Teacher or Head of the School. If ...lty should be found in answering any of the questions, application should be made to the Trustees or ...gers (where the School is under the government of such officers) and the information procured from them.

It is requested that, before filling up the Form, the Instructions, on the last page, as to the proper manner of ...so, may be perused; and that a rough draft of the answers may first be made, and then fairly copied into the ...

Proprietors of strictly private establishments are not required to answer questions 11, 13, and 14.

Superintendent Registrar's District	Registrar's District	Parish, or Township, or Extra Parochial Place
Keighley Union	*Bingley*	*Township of Bingley.*

1. ...e and Locality of School? *(See Instruction, 1.)* — *National School, Cullingworth*

2. ...at which the School was Established? *(See Instruction, 2.)* — *August. 1848.*

3. ...e School held in a Building legally ...cured in trust for purposes of ...ducation? — *Yes.*

4. ...e School the Private Establishment ...the Teacher? or is the Teacher ap...inted by, or subject to, any, and ...at, Governors? — *Trustees*

5. ...e School has any other Governors ...an the Teacher, are these Governors ...pointed under any Trust Deed, ...arter, or Act of Parliament? — *Trust Deed*

EDUCATIONAL RETURN.
(Prepared under the direction of one of Her Majesty's Principal Secretaries of State.)

(A.)

1851

Census of Great Britain.

... PRECEDING RETURN.

...ification of the School should be om... a *Grammar* School, Mr. Smith's *prin...* ..., as the case may require.

...lty arises from remoteness of time, th... the earliest date at which it can be re...

...ormitories, Day-rooms, Studies, Eati... ...ing School hours, are *not* to be returned.

...ho are actually paying for instruction a... ...School.

...ay have been no School held on March... ...ss may be entered; the requisite altern...

...ith that in column 3.

...be inserted the Total Amount received...

Figure 4
Education returns for the registration district of Keighley, Yorks, 1851 (HO 129/494)

Figure 5
Milton Board School Orchestral Class, 1903 (COPY 1/160)

adult evening classes and Sunday schools. The existence of an educational return for a given place can be established only by examination of the relevant bundle of ecclesiastical returns, since there is no separate index. In the absence of an individual return, the abstract *Report of the Commissioners for taking a Census of Great Britain on Education* (HC 1852-3 xc) contains details of attendances, ages of pupils, numbers, type and capacity of schools, with totals for the whole registration or poor law district. The published 1851 Education census does not give information on individual schools, though where there was only one particular type in a registration district it may thus be identifiable from other sources.

A Royal Commission was appointed in 1858 'to inquire into the present state of popular education in England'. The report of this Commission, chaired by the Duke of Newcastle, was issued in 1861 (HC 1861 xxi). Surviving papers of the commission are in T 74/1-2, including minutes and correspondence of assistant commissioners. While the Newcastle Commission was deliberating, Robert Lowe, the new vice-president of the Committee of Council on Education, was revising the minutes of the PCCE so that relevant regulations about grants and other important matters could be printed in one volume; this was issued as the Code of 1860 (ED 17/1). The combination of the recommendations of the Newcastle Commission and the efforts of Robert Lowe, who produced a Revised Code in 1862, culminated in a system of payment by results, with government grant dependent on average attendance and examination performance, tested by Her Majesty's inspectors. Lowe justified the new system by claiming in a speech reported in *Hansard* in February 1862 'If it is not cheap, it shall be efficient; if it is not efficient it shall be cheap'.

Increasing dissatisfaction with the state of elementary education led to a parliamentary investigation into conditions in Liverpool, Manchester, Leeds and Birmingham in 1869 by J G Fitch and D R Fearon (HC 1870 liv). It sought to show that the facilities for elementary education were woefully inadequate and that improvement was hampered by religious controversy.

The application of government funds to popular education from 1833 exacerbated the 'religious difficulty'. Throughout the nineteenth century views differed on what or whether religious teaching should be given in state-aided schools. There were those who thought that national education should be a major duty of the established church, ie the Church of England. This was the opinion of the National Society. Another voluntary body, well supported by Nonconformists, the British and Foreign Society, aided schools open to any denomination and which gave no distinctive sectarian teaching.

Twelve files survive in ED 48 of associations of voluntary elementary schools formed to administer grant-aid under the Voluntary Schools Act 1897.

3.5 Elementary Education Act 1870 (Forster Act)

The aim of this act, introduced by W E Forster, vice-president of the Education Department, was to 'fill in the gaps'. Popular instruction before 1870 was catered for by a system of government inspected, partially state financed but otherwise independent, voluntary schools. Files on elementary schools in receipt of annual grants or accorded temporary government approval are in ED 21. These files contain statistics, information about school premises, trusts, accommodation, inspection and organization.

Forster's Act required locally elected school boards to provide elementary schools where existing facilities were inadequate. ED 9/22 contains material on the election of members of school boards between 1871 and 1891, including voting papers. Provision was made for the possible transfer of voluntary schools to school board control. Files on both types of school are in ED 21 and among the Parish Files (ED 2). ED 4 contains files on schools transferred to the London School Board. Section 61 of the act provided for a census to be taken to establish the existing school provision. The subsequent returns survive in ED 2 for parishes with no school or more than one, ED 21 for parishes with only one school, ED 3 for London schools and ED 16 for municipal boroughs.

EXAMPLE:

Parish File for Farnham (ED 2/426) shows the following grant-aided schools in the parish in 1871:

name of school	nos accom				in receipt
	B	G	Inf	Total	annual grant
Tilford CE (mixed)				96	yes
Farnham National School	212	183		395	yes
Farnham Infant School	(60 on books)		135		yes
Farnham British School	(210 on books)			290	yes
Hale CE (mixed)	(300 on books)			257	yes
Wrecclesham NS (mixed)	(300 on books)			243	yes

Section 7(1) of the act contained the compromise reached to meet the differences in approach by religious teaching; it was known as the Cowper-Temple clause. By this clause school boards were left to decide whether their schools should give religious

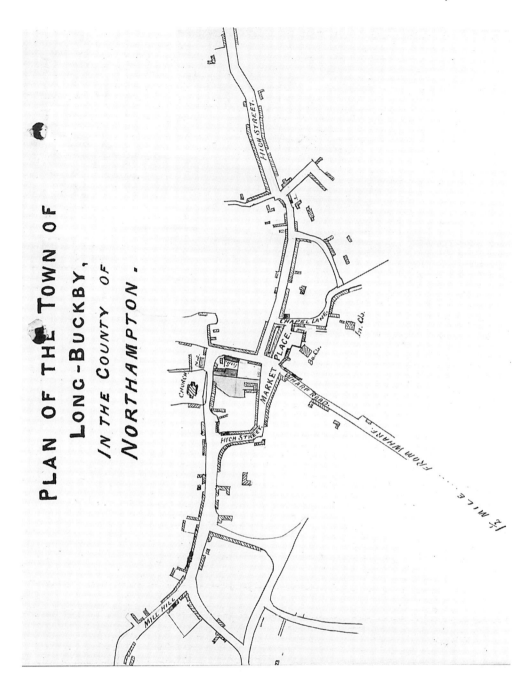

Figure 6
Plan of Long Buckley, Northants, showing roads, buildings, church and school,
?late 19thC (ED 2/331)

instruction, but if it was provided, 'no religious catechism or religious formulary which is distinctive of any particular denomination shall be taught'. Moreover, a conscience clause was added which permitted parents to withdraw a child from religious instruction if they so wished.

The 1870 Act thus created a dual system; part board schools, undenominational and supported by government grants, rates and fees; part denominational schools without rate-aid but with government grants, fees, subscriptions and endowments. Under section five of the Elementary Education Act 1891, provision was made for free schooling. ED 9/16 contains a summary of applications under this section between 1892 and 1894 and specimens of claim forms. A separate series of free education files was created of which the following specimen files were retained and placed on the supply files in ED 16:

Place	Former reference	Current reference
Enfield	P/S 26 (5) G	ED 16/209
Gravesend	E 19 (185) G	ED 16/118
Birkenhead	P/S 54 G	ED 16/23-24
Lincoln	P/S 90 G	ED 16/200
Liverpool	P/S 91 G	ED 16/166
Willesden	P/S 26 (16) G	ED 16/217-220
Preston	P/S 102 G	ED 16/182

The Cross Commission was appointed in 1886 to assess elementary education since the 1870 Act. There was disagreement over recommendations and a majority report was produced (HC 1888 xxxv, xxxvi; some working papers in ED 10/42). The main points of dispute were: the religious issue - whether voluntary schools should be aided from the rates; and the meaning of elementary - some school boards were financing so called higher grade schools.

3.5.1   Higher Grade and Higher Elementary Schools

The Cross Commission highlighted the problem of catering for children of thirteen plus. Different solutions had been developed. In 1872, for example, the Leeds School Board established the first higher grade school. Other large towns and cities including London followed this precedent and by 1894 there were sixty-three such schools. Another response was for elementary schools to develop 'higher tops', classes where pupils who had passed through standard VII were taught more advanced work. Most higher grade schools eventually became secondary schools.

After April 1900 Higher Elementary Schools were recognized by the Board of Education. These schools included in their curriculum a graduated course in elementary science for children between ten and fifteen. Files on these schools survive in ED 20. The papers on these files reflect the careful scrutiny and supervision of these schools after the Cockerton Judgment (*see 2.3*) and the consultations with the Science and Art Department.

3.5.2   Institution Schools

ED 30 contains institution school files (in England only) mostly relating to schools held in orphanages.

eg   'Indefatigable' Training Ship School   1875-1914   ED 30/42
      Stepney: 62 Burdett Road, Leopold House
                  Dr Barnardo's Home School   1884-1909   ED 30/62

3.6   Independent Schools

Information is available on schools outside the state sector. Some files survive among the Privy Council Unbound Papers (PC 1) relating to the administration of charitable trusts for independent elementary schools (PC 1/2684-2692).

Papers on private and independent schools recognized by the Education Department as efficient under the varying definitions of the term since 1871 are in ED 33; not all such files have been preserved. About a tenth of the files in ED 33 contain the Parish File (otherwise in ED 2) where the parish only contained one school in 1871 and that an independent school. Returns of schools not recognized for grant or efficiency under the Education Acts of 1918 and 1921 are in ED 15.

3.7   Poor Law Schools

Poor Law schools were provided and maintained by the guardians of the poor, either attached to workhouses or as separate schools. The parliamentary grant was extended to workhouse schools in 1846. Records of the fourteen district schools (run jointly by several poor law unions in or for predominantly urban areas), first established in 1849, are in MH 27. Correspondence about workhouse schools run by individual unions will be found in MH 12 and MH 32.

In 1904 inspection of the educational and industrial work of these schools was transferred to the Board of Education from the Local Government Board. The surviving poor law school files are in ED 132. Under the Local Government Act 1929 educational provision for poor law children became the responsibility of the local authorities. In many areas these children already attended public elementary schools; existing poor law schools were formally converted into public elementary schools. The London County Council, however, continued to administer residential schools and homes established by boards of guardians. Local authority schemes for the education of poor law children between 1929 and 1944 are in ED 95. (*See also 10.1.1.*)

3.8   Industrial, Reformatory and Works Schools

The term 'industrial' school referred to different kinds of schools at different times. The eighteenth century saw the development of schools of industry, where pauper children were taught from a very young age to spin, wind, plait straw, sew, cobble and garden. The sale of their products went towards the upkeep of the school. These schools often had some slight academic input, usually religious teaching but sometimes also reading. A return of 1809 in the *Report of the Society for bettering the Condition of the Poor* shows that of the 188,794 children between five and fourteen receiving parish relief only 20,336 were in schools of industry with some minimal education.

The state was not involved in the foundation or running of such schools and thus the incidence of information about these charity schools among the public records is rare and haphazard. The class of building plans (ED 228) contains a description of an industrial school in Chardstock in Dorset (ED 228/76). It is a three page printed pamphlet describing the work of the school, which developed from its foundation in 1849 as a training establishment for ten girls to be prepared for service, into an orphan school for industry educating ninety girls and boys, orphans of the Crimean War. A suitable portion of the day was set aside for their mental, moral and religious development by a certificated master and mistress. They were also taught to perform everyday duties and the 'common arts of domestic life': domestic service for the girls and gardening for the boys. Most of the money for this venture came from the Patriotic Fund but its promoters were also seeking some money from the PCCE, hence the pamphlet.

During the nineteenth century, with the increase in legislation limiting the numbers of hours children could work, schools were set up adjacent to factories to provide some elementary education for the young employees. The Chancery Masters Exhibits (evidence submitted in cases in the Court of Chancery) happen to include the attendance books and time books for Bottoms School covering the years 1838-1841. This school was provided for the children employed in the mill of Messrs R Law and Co at Ramsden in Rochdale (C 106/44).

From the mid-nineteenth century central government departments became responsible for certain aspects of both industrial and reformatory schools. In 1857 the PCCE

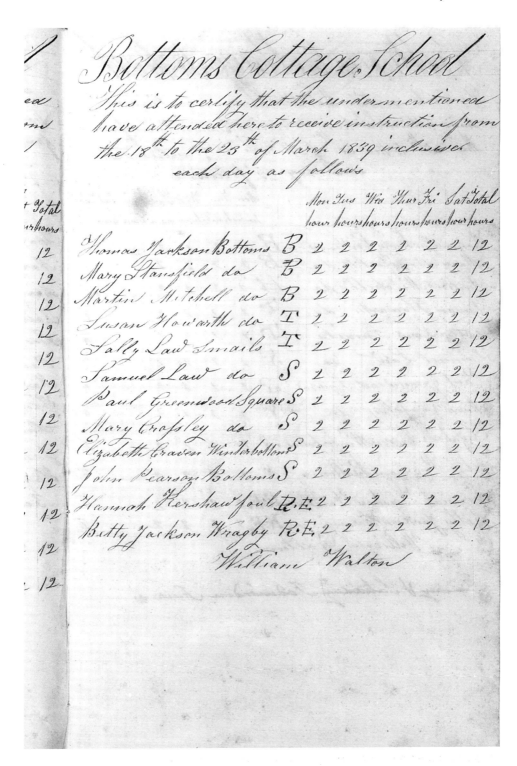

Figure 7
Attendance books for Bottoms industrial school, 1838-1841 (C 106/44)

was given powers of certification and inspection over industrial schools but three years later these responsibilities were transferred to the Home Office. That department already had the right to certify, inspect and give money to reformatory schools. By 1866 the Reformatory and Industrial Department of the Home Office was established. After the Children's Act 1908 a departmental committee on reformatory and industrial schools recommended in 1913 that a special branch of the Home Office be formed to deal with all administrative and inspecting functions of the department relating to children.

A Children's Branch was finally set up in 1924 and from that time reformatory and industrial schools were replaced by remand homes and approved schools. HO 45 contains the general correspondence of the Reformatory and Industrial Schools Department, with out-letters about the schools in HO 13, HO 136 and HO 137. Correspondence and papers of the Inspectorate of the Children's Department are in HO 360, HO 361 and HO 366. Information about expenditure on approved schools is in HO 362 and registers and other records of these schools and remand homes are in HO 349.

3.9   Education Act 1902 (Balfour Act)

This act put education under local authority control, without abolishing the dual system of board and religious schools. 2,559 school boards and 788 school attendance committees were replaced by 330 local education authorities (LEAs). All the former board schools and most of the British and Nonconformist voluntary schools were transferred to the LEAs and became provided schools. Private Office Papers relating to the bill are in ED 24 code 7/8.

R L Morant, secretary to the Board of Education, introduced a new Elementary School Code in 1904:

> The purpose of the Public Elementary School is to form and strengthen the character and to develop the intelligence of the children entrusted to it, and to make the best use of the school years available, in assisting both girls and boys, according to their different needs, to fit themselves, practically as well as intellectually, for the work of life.

Individual elementary school files continued to be maintained by central government after the creation of LEAs. These files are in ED 21. They are arranged in four series alphabetically by county, then within each county, where applicable, alphabetically by county borough and boroughs.

When schools were taken on to the Annual Grant List they were given a number in a single country-wide series. The first alphabetical sequence of schools in ED 21 (pieces

1-754) follows this numeration and relates to schools closed before 1906. That year a new system of numbering began which gave each LEA a separate series starting at 1. The remaining files in ED 21 are arranged in three separate alphabetical series using the new numeration. In order to find all the files for a particular school you need to look at each alphabetical sequence of counties.

Eg Farnham, Surrey

ED 21/542	1893	Bourne Road School - former St Thomas C of E School	no 18348
ED 21/16916	1892-1912	Farnham C of E School	no 121
ED 21/40582	1924	Farnham C of E School	no 121
ED 21/61706	1936-1937	Farnham C of E School	no 121

Other schools are also listed under Farnham because, as the town expanded, more school places were needed, but you will know you have the same school by checking the school number.

The new numbering system was used retrospectively for the preliminary statements (ED 7). Each box of statements contains a numbered list of the schools using the post-1906 system. The statements for Farnham (ED 7/118) include one for Farnham National School which has 121 on it in green crayon. That particular statement was completed in 1896 but it gives the date of the current buildings as 1860 (the date of the building grant referred to at 3.3).

When the Board of Education took over the powers of the Charity Commissioners in 1899 it inherited the files of the commissioners on endowed schools. Those relating exclusively to elementary schools are in ED 49, which thus contains Charity Commission papers, observations by the Education Department on educational matters referred by the Commissioners before 1899 as well as material on the subsequent administration of these schools by the Board. Papers concerning endowments of school premises are often interrelated with the school files in ED 21.

The Board of Education introduced school history sheets in the 1920s and they were discontinued by the DES in 1983. They recorded, in summary form, details about each school in England maintained by LEAs. These details included the name, location, status and size of the school, and the sex and age range of its pupils. The date of establishment was also required. For voluntary schools information about ownership of the premises was often supplied. Building projects in prospect and other details about the school or its organization also appear. The history sheets are in ED 185 but are arranged by geographical location, LEA and date, with those for 1900-1983 kept together in a block; thus they are not yet open to public inspection.

3.10   Local Education Authorities

Local education authorities (LEAs) were created by the Education Act 1902. Before this the education authority could be the school board, formed after 1870, the school managers, the parish council or any other local body with educational responsibilities.

3.10.1   School Attendance

Nineteenth century factory and mines acts regulating child labour also contained educational provisions. Since 1853 elementary schools had received a capitation grant based on the number of pupils in average attendance and the inspectorate, who were responsible for ensuring that grants were not abused, emphasized the merits of regular attendance. Legislation in 1855 gave poor law guardians the option of making parental receipt of out relief conditional on school attendance for the children. The inspectorate reviewed school attendance in their reports in 1869 (HC 1870 xxli). The Forster Act did not make attendance compulsory; it enabled school boards to make bye-laws to compel attendance and to appoint school attendance officers to enforce it.

Under Section 7 of the Elementary Education Act 1876 (Lord Sandon's Act), school attendance committees could be set up in districts where there were no school boards. ED 6 contains papers relating to the formation and business of these Union School Attendance Committees. The Education Act 1880 (Mundella's Act) made the framing of attendance bye-laws compulsory for all school boards and school attendance committees; attendance was made obligatory for children between five and ten. Legislation in 1918 further restricted the employment of children and the 1921 Education Act made education compulsory up to fourteen.

The Attendance Files (ED 18) contain information on various aspects of school attendance including bye-laws authorized under the 1870 Act, exemption certificates, the Factory Acts, 'half time scholars', etc. A file of correspondence with Liverpool CBC (ED 18/143) includes discussion of a claim made in July 1879 that the suicide of Samuel Williams was:

> caused by being out of work and the pressure the School Board
> had put upon him in respect to sending his children to school.

Other aspects of school attendance are dealt with in the code files in ED 19 and papers relating to attendance in parishes before 1903 are on the Parish Files in ED 2.

3.10.2   School Boards

There is no single series of correspondence with individual school boards. ED 14, the London General Files, contains papers on the general problems confronting the London School Board in the implementation of educational legislation. Local Government Board correspondence relating to the audit and financial control of London School Board expenditure for the period 1871 to 1905 is available (MH 27/ 130-142). The School Board Office files (ED 57) relate to the site of such offices and only then if attached to a Pupil-Teacher Centre and not to any school board functions. Petitions by school boards and later LEAs for the compulsory purchase of land for schools are in ED 5 until 1919, and thereafter on the schools files (*see 3.11*).

3.10.3   Parish Files

The Parish Files (ED 2) contain correspondence on attendance and school accommodation with school boards of parishes not included in a borough or in the metropolis. The series relates to those parishes in which there was no school or more than one in 1870. There are two other places to look for parish files: where there was only one school the papers have either been absorbed into the ED 21 file for that parish or they have gone into ED 33 with material on independent schools and are marked in that list with an asterisk.

3.10.4   Accommodation or 'Supply' Files

Under the 1902 Act LEAs assumed the duties of the school boards and board schools became council schools. They took on responsibility for the maintenance but not the provision of voluntary or non-provided schools. The Supply Files (ED 16) were made up after 1903 and relate to the supply of elementary school accommodation by the LEAs established under 1902 Act. In the case of county councils, the files began no earlier than 1902 but the files for county boroughs and for municipal boroughs and urban districts, designated Part III Authorities under the act, contain earlier correspondence with school boards and school districts superseded or taken over by those authorities. They also contain surviving papers from the earlier Free Education and Poor Law series of files. The Local Education Authority Code Files relating to the administration of Codes of Regulations 1903 to 1921 (ED 19) include some information on school attendance, staffing and grant approval.

3.10.5   Other LEA Files

LEAs' applications for grants (made under the 1918 and 1921 Acts) were carefully scrutinized. The Board of Education maintained precedent files on these grants (ED 88) which contain examples of both parsimony and extravagance on the part of certain LEAs. The series was discontinued after the Education Act 1944 when revised financial provisions were introduced.

The Education Act 1902 (section 17) required LEAs to set up education committees. The files in ED 139 contain schemes for these committees submitted for Board of Education approval. The number of LEAs was greatly reduced by the Butler Act 1944, when most non-county borough and urban district LEAs were absorbed into their respective county authority. The files are arranged in alphabetical order of counties and county boroughs, with a separate series at the end of the list relating to Greater London Boroughs created under the London Government Act 1963.

ED 89 contains files on extra-district children, those living within the jurisdiction of one LEA but educated in another. Wider aspects of the administration of elementary education from 1903, not common to the subject files, are dealt with in the Local Education Authority Miscellaneous Files (ED 111).

3.10.6   Burston Strike School

Sometimes the dealings of one LEA could have far-reaching consequences as in the case of Burston in Norfolk. Here in 1914 a playground incident involving three young children became a weapon in a bitter dispute between the local education authority, the school managers and the Christian Socialist teachers, Mr and Mrs Higden, leading to the dismissal of the latter (for allegedly beating pupils) and their establishment of a separate school known as the Burston Strike School, which lasted until 1939. It was a notorious affair which split the local community and in which labour, social and political organizations all over the country became interested. The school file for that period has been left unweeded and is in three parts (ED 21/12712B).

3.11   Hadow Reports

The Board of Education Act 1899 created a Consultative Committee to advise the Board of Education. During the inter-war period it issued several influential reports, some of which were concerned with elementary education. They were known as the Hadow Reports after the name of the chairman Sir Henry Hadow. The first report *Education and the Adolescent* was published in 1926. It proposed that primary education should end at eleven plus; the term 'elementary' should disappear. ED 97 contains files on the consequent reorganization of schools to provide a system of advanced elementary education. Working papers of the Committee are in ED 10/147 and ED 24/1265.

1931 saw the issue of a separate report on *The Primary School* (papers ED 10/148). It advocated the use of 'activity' based teaching in primary schools, recommended two distinct phases in primary education: before seven and from seven to eleven, and endorsed the clean break at eleven.

3.12   Education in wartime

Before the declaration of war, large numbers of children were moved from urban areas thought to be targets of future enemy air attacks to safe places known as reception areas. The organization of national education under these conditions was very difficult and numerous children escaped the system. Evacuation was voluntary and many children returned home, buildings were often inadequate or non existent, improvization and ingenuity were employed by both teachers and schools inspectors and different methods of teaching evolved to meet the altered conditions.

Any search for information about wartime education should begin with ED 138. This class contains draft chapters of an official history of education in the war. The work was undertaken by Dr Sophia Weitzman but was uncompleted at her death in 1965 (but was made available to P H J H Gosden for his book *Education in the Second World War*). The original plan was for two volumes: the first to contain chapters covering the impact of defence preparations on education to 1939, a review of the war years, followed by special studies on nutrition, medical services, under fives, and the employment of children in agriculture; the second volume was intended as a survey of the growth of state education culminating in a detailed discussion of the 1944 Act.

Code 16 of the General Education, General Files (ED 10) contains papers relating to education during the war. ED 10/252 deals with the scope of the Board of Education's history of public education in wartime, including reports on home classes and activities for women. The Board issued a series of pamphlets under the title *Schools in Wartime* covering a wide range of subject matter, from 'The use of Ordnance Survey Maps' to 'Teaching First Aid in the Schools' and illustrating the flexible approach to teaching which was adopted at the time. Copies of these pamphlets are in ED 10/286. Files also survive on camp schools constructed and administered by the National Camps Corporation Limited, set up and funded under the Camps Act 1939. The schools were built in rural areas to cater for evacuees. Policy papers are in ED 10/235-242A and ED 11/192, 193, 299 and six complete representative specimen camp school files are available (ED 134/248-253). One file also survives on arrangements in Wales for children from 'the special areas' (ED 92/21). ED 66 contains a series of files concerning provision for nursery age children of women war workers (ED 66/59-145).

Information about the response of individual local authorities to the educational problems posed by the Second World War is available in ED 134, arranged alphabetically by authority. All files on refugees in schools and reports by His Majesty's Inspectors (HMI) on war evacuation have been preserved.

3.13   Education Act 1944 (Butler Act)

The whole process of evacuation had a profound effect on attitudes towards education. Early in the war discussions began about educational reconstruction. In 1941 a memorandum called the Green Book 'was distributed in such a blaze of secrecy that it achieved an unusual degree of publicity' (ED 136/212-301). It stimulated wide-ranging debate on post-war education. The Green Book consultative exercise together with the Hadow and Spens Reports, supplemented by the work of the Norwood Committee (*see chapter 11.6*), resulted in the Education Act 1944 (Bill Papers ED 31/500-548, Private Office Papers ED 136/377-541).

Under this act public education was to be organized in three progressive stages: primary (replacing elementary), secondary and further education. Records of individual primary schools will be found in ED 161. These files contain information similar to that in ED 21 and continue to 1966; they cover only counties A-K. Under section 11(1) LEAs were required to submit development plans for their areas covering both primary and secondary schools. The results of their work are in ED 152, where the files include protests against the plans, mainly over the closing or amalgamation of schools.

EXAMPLE:

The files for Norfolk are particularly full (ED 152/115-118, 470-475). They include information about the submission of the development plan for the local area, exhaustive discussion of the proposals, a lengthy memo from the chief education officer and detailed maps of each part of the county showing the position of individual schools. ED 152/117 is the protest file for the county. It includes a letter from the rector of Caistor St Edmund stating that the plan 'proposes a general massacre of the church schools in Norfolk'. The file also contains a petition from South Runcton voluntary primary Church of England school which was 'signed by almost the entire village, and represents 97.5% of the total number asked'. It was addressed to the Minister of Education:

> While fully appreciating the objects of the Norfolk Education
> Committee's Plan as submitted to you, we feel that it has been
> drawn up with reference rather to a map than the needs and well
> being of our community.

Under the Butler Act, the Consultative Committee was replaced by an Advisory Council (*see 4.8 below*). One of its most influential post-war reports was *Children and their Primary Schools*, published in 1967 under the chairmanship of Lady Plowden and usually known as the *Plowden Report*. It recommended dividing primary education into two stages, five to eight and eight to twelve; equalizing educational opportunities by giving deprived areas the best schools; child centred learning and an integrated curriculum. Records of the council relating to this inquiry are in ED 146/64-93 and ED 207/1-14.

3.14 Elementary School Case Study - Bebington National School, Cheshire

This study draws on the various types of document outlined in this chapter to show how the history of schools in a given area can be traced from an entry in the *Digest of Parochial Returns* for 1819 to the School Digest Files (ED 161) with papers from the 1960s. It started as the study of a single school known as Bebington National School in Cheshire but for some purposes it also mentions the National Society school at New Ferry in the same parish. It seems that at certain times the Education Department was confused over which school number to assign to each school. This example was also chosen to fit in with the study of inspectorate reports for the same area (*see 10.5.2-3*).

Document	Reference	Description
1819 *Digest*	HC 1819 ix	*Digest of Parochial Returns* first state survey of elementary school provision taken in 1816
Trust Deeds	C 54/12734 C 54/14945 C 54/15556	deed enrolled 1842 deed enrolled 1856 deed enrolled 1860
Building Grants	ED 103/135 ED 103/98	Lower Bebington 1835 New Ferry 1860
Endowment Files	ED 49/659 ED 49/660 ED 49/11416	New Ferry 1928 School Lands Foundation 1855 -1934 School Lands Foundation 1936-38

Document	Reference	Description
Preliminary Statements	ED 7/6	Lower Bebington, Bebington National and New Ferry
Parish File	ED 2/39	Lower Bebington
Inspectors' Reports mid 19th century examples - *see 10.5.2 for extracts relating to Bebington*	ED 17/8 ED 17/10 ED 17/11 ED 17/19	1845 1847 1849 1853
School Files	ED 21/1828 ED 21/24402 ED 21/47962	1894-1912 1920-1937 1938
Inspectors' Reports early 20th century examples - *see 10.5.5 for extracts relating to Bebington*	ED 21/24402 ED 21/47962	1920,1923, 1927,1931 1938
Post-Hadow reorganization	ED 97/16 ED 97/31	Major File 1925-1935 Wirral (central and Ellesmere Port) 1928-1932
Development Plans post 1944	ED 152/13-16	1945-1956
Inspectors' Reports post 1944 - *see 10.5.6 for extract*	ED 156/5	1-2 Nov 1951
School History Sheet	ED 185	not yet open
School Digest File	ED 161/1602	1951-1964

3.14.1   Digest of Parochial Returns 1819

The Digest (HC 1819 x) contains an entry for Bebington, stating that it consists of Higher and Lower Bebington, Poulton with Spittle, Storeton and Tranmere. The parish contains one school in which about 20 or 30 children are taught. The salary of the teacher is £25 arising from endowment of the land.

3.14.2   Trust Deeds C 54

The topographical index to trust deeds up to 1870 contains three entries under Bebington. The close roll entries show that Sir Thomas Stanley of Hooton Park conveyed 285 square yards of land in Lower Bebington for a house and National School by an indenture dated 16 May 1836. The deed was enrolled 4 April 1842 (C 54/12734, entry nos 15 and 16). George Orred of Tranmere made provision in his will to convey 3060 square acres of land to Bebington National School; the close roll entry includes a coloured plan of the land specified. The deed was enrolled on 3 May 1856 (C 54/14945, entry no 8). Four years later William Hope of Wavertree voluntarily granted 1248 square yards of pasture land at New Ferry for a school for the village. He laid down detailed instructions about its management which are included in the deed together with a plan of the site. The deed was enrolled 20 December 1860 (C 54/15556, entry no 9).

3.14.3   Endowment Files ED 49

In 1855 the Secretary of State received a letter from Reverend Feilden, the Rector of Bebington, stating that the local school was inadequate for the wants of the parish and was fast falling out of repair (ED 49/660). Since the endowment produced only £26 per annum in income and precluded them from asking for voluntary aid, the only way to raise the money necessary to rectify the situation was by sale of mortgage. Feilden wanted the Charity Commissioners to authorize a mortgage of £500. Later papers contained in the Endowment File reveal that the school lands were sold to the Lever Brothers in 1892 for the sum of £7473 16s 6d which was invested in various stocks and shares producing an income of £220 per annum. However, a dispute regarding the distribution of this money arose in 1905 when an application for an Order establishing a Scheme for the Administration of the Bebington School Lands was submitted. It was argued by Mr Lever MP that the scheme should also include schools in Higher Bebington, not just those in Lower Bebington. However, after a detailed inquiry, it was decided that the original beneficiary of the trust was Lower Bebington and this could not be altered. Details of the original endowment and the correspondence surrounding the dispute can be found in ED 49/660.

The New Ferry School in Lower Bebington was also at the centre of a dispute in 1928. The Secretary of State received a letter from Walter Peel, the trustee of a legacy providing money for school prizes, seeking advice regarding the transfer of

LIVERPOOL JOHN MOORES UNIVERSITY
LEARNING SERVICES

the trust to the Vicar and Churchwardens (ED 49/659). This apparently simple request was complicated by the terms of the original endowment. The Vicar of New Ferry, J Milton Thompson, argued that the legacy was left to benefit the children who attended parish schools and was, therefore, denominational in nature. It was his contention that the money should be used to benefit the children who attended the local Sunday school. After careful consideration, however, the Board decided that all children attending schools in the parish were to benefit and that a scheme should be established to administer the legacy.

3.14.4 Building Grants ED 103

The index to the building grant papers confirms that there were applications for two National Society schools in Bebington. Papers relating to the first one in 1835 (ED 103/135, pp 185-188) consist of a memorial from the promoters of the school dated 27 April 1835 and an abstract of correspondence between the National Society and the clergy and inhabitants of Lower Bebington. The chief correspondent is the Rev Mosley Feilden, rector of Bebington. The abstract refers to existing day school provision for 20 boys and 10 girls. This could be the school referred to in the *Digest*.

There is more information about the application for the school at New Ferry (ED 103/98, pp 413-431). The papers include a memorial on a pre-printed form signed by the chief promoters, Reverend Feilden, Rector of Bebington, among them. This is followed by Building Form no 7: a set of questions about the tenure of the proposed site, to be completed by a solicitor, signed on 20 March 1860 by a Liverpool firm of solicitors; details of the dimensions of the proposed buildings to be accompanied by building plans, signed by Thomas C Clarke, an architect; and a summary of the estimated costs. Building Form 7a is a list of local contributors, seventy-four in all, with their addresses, rateable value of their property and their contribution. Finally there is a certificate signed by the majority of the subscribers' committee and the school management committee confirming that the work has been carried out, that the school is open with teachers appointed, signed 31 March 1862. A balance sheet showing the final cost of the work is attached.

3.14.5 Preliminary Statements ED 7

The parish of Bebington was very close to the expanding Birkenhead and Port Sunlight, where Mr Lever set up his model village. These areas all required elementary schools. It seems that in the initial allocation of school numbers by the Education Department this area was omitted. In the list of schools at the beginning of the box of preliminary statements for Cheshire (ED 7/6) the Bebington and Port Sunlight schools are given the numbers 34A to 34E and appear to be an addition.

Two preliminary statements are pinned together for Lower Bebington School and Bebington National School. The first statement has the school number 169 in green crayon crossed out and the number 34A added in red in a triangle. The statement for Lower Bebington school seems to be that one referred to in the first set of building grant application papers, with the earlier trust deed. Its school buildings were erected in 1837 and the preliminary statement is dated 14 September 1848. The statement pinned to it for Bebington National School gives details of a school built in 1856 with a trust deed of the same year. There is also a preliminary statement for New Ferry school built in 1861 but no details of the trust deed. This statement has the school number 34E written on it, with 170 crossed out.

There are no sketch plans of the buildings on any of these preliminary statements and no plans for Bebington schools in ED 228.

3.14.6   Parish Files ED 2

The Parish File for Bebington (ED 2/39) contains an inspector's report on the township of Lower Bebington carried out in 1872 in accordance with the Forster Act 1870. It confirms that there are two schools in the area: New Ferry C of E and Bebington National C of E. The file also contains correspondence with the Lower Bebington School Board in 1891-1892 about setting up a School Attendance Committee.

The 1902 Education Act caused the new Local Education Authority to consider setting up a Public Higher Elementary School and the resulting correspondence, including a proposed curriculum and a preliminary statement, is on the file. The Parish File also contains a 'model district report' by the local HMI about the schools in the Bebington district, which the Board of Education considers worth copying to the Cheshire Education Authority *(for further details see HMI Reports Case Study 10.5.4).*

3.14.7   HMI Reports 1840-1899

Between 1840 and 1899 HMI reports were printed for Parliament as part of the annual report of the Education Department and rarely contain detailed reports for individual schools. The printed versions consist of general reports for the counties for which a district or divisional inspector was responsible. No full manuscript reports from individual inspectors survive among the records of the PCCE or the Education Department. Extracts relating to Bebington National School from the printed reports are given in 10.5.2.

3.14.8   School Files ED 21

The School Files in ED 21 continue to use the school number, in this case 34A and 169. There are four series of files in ED 21 arranged alphabetically by county, three of them should contain files for a particular school. If it was closed before 1906 its file will be in the first series. The files have been heavily weeded.

The earliest file for Bebington is ED 21/1828. The surviving papers cover the years 1894 to 1911 and include: a plan and correspondence about the enlargement of the cloakroom; discussion on whether the school is compelled to take a pupil when it is already full; and information about an additional classroom for fifty infants. The school managers raise the question of who can fix school holidays after the establishment of an LEA. They also argue to retain the name 'National' but the Board insists that 'Church of England' should be used.

The file also contains details of a new scheme for 'foundation' lands granted by deed of 11 February 1855 and now to be applied to both Bebington C of E and Lower Bebington New Ferry C of E schools. The provisions in the trust deed of 13 March 1856 are also considered in a discussion about the use of the school premises out of hours, involving the responsibility for repairs.

The next file is ED 21/24402. The file cover has the school number 34A but inside the school is numbered 169. The surviving contents are HMI reports as follows:

Name of school	Date	School Number
Lower Bebington Church of England, boys school	1920	169
Bebington, Bromborough, Bebington C of E whole school	1923	34A
Bebington, Bromborough, Bebington C of E boys school	1927	34A
ditto, girls school	1927	34A
ditto, infants school	1927	34A
Lower Bebington C of E	1931	34A

The third series of school files also includes one for Bebington (ED 21/47962). It contains an HMI report for 1938 for Bebington C of E school (number 34A).

3.14.9   Post-Hadow Reorganization ED 97

ED 97/16 and 31. A deputation from Cheshire Education Authority visited the Board of Education on 11 February 1927 to discuss advanced instruction in Cheshire schools. The major file (ED 97/16) contains details of this meeting and a report on the reorganization in Cheshire. For Bebington it is proposed that the C of E primary school is retained with a new council primary school on the ground floor of the Church Road site and a new modern school, ie for 'advanced' instruction, is to occupy the upper floor of that building.

ED 97/31 relates almost entirely to the Bebington and Bromborough schools. Discussions continued throughout the summer of 1931 between the Board and the LEA about the details of the reorganization in the Bebington and Bromborough area. The Board was concerned that the proposals meant that some children would not experience a 'break' at eleven plus as recommended in the Hadow Report of 1931 because they would be staying in the same building. Eventually the Board approved the proposals but only on the 'understanding that the arrangements will be regarded as temporary'.

The LEA proposals for Bebington C. E. School were:

> Lower Bebington C. E. School will be a Primary School (Infants and Juniors), with accommodation for 317 children and will be in charge of one Head Teacher.

The Board received the following advice from HMI Arnold about the school:

> Of the existing schools Lower Bebington C. E. is nearly full on paper and overcrowded in fact ... but I do not expect any material increase in the number of children in this area during the next two years.

3.14.10 Development Plans ED 152

Following the Education Act 1944, LEAs were asked to draw up plans for primary and secondary education in their areas. ED 152/13-16, 441 are the relevant files for Cheshire.

ED 152/13 contains a copy of the printed development plan for the county. The Bebington schools come under the Bebington Divisional Executive No 1 (pp 7-11). The scheme as planned does not include school number 34A. It is listed as Bebington CE (34A) under 'Primary and Secondary Schools to be Discontinued'. Its pupils are to be transferred to the new County Primary Schools at Bebington Old Chester Road. There are two files of protests to the Development Plan for Cheshire schools (ED 152/14 and 15). The second one (ED 152/15) contains a protest from the managers of Lower Bebington C of E school. In November 1951, on a pre-printed form, commonly used for such requests, they ask the Minister of Education for 'Aided' status and register an objection to the proposed closure of the school. A letter from the Cheshire Education Committee, dated 30 July 1952, informs the Ministry that the school managers have objected and adds:

> There are at present 264 children of Primary School age on roll. The Authority proposes that the children displaced from this school, together with children from the new housing development should be accommodated in the new 2-form entry County Infants and new 2-form entry County Junior School on the Bebington Oval site.

This letter is followed by one from the Ministry to the Lower Bebington school managers, stamped 13 Nov 1953, stating:

> The Minister has supported your objection to the Plan which in general she has now approved and the Managers may expect in due course to be consulted by the Diocesan Education Committee and the Local Education Authority about recent proposals for the future of the school.

ED 152/16 includes detailed sections on the special conditions and requirements of each Divisional Executive; Bebington is No 1.

3.14.11 Post -1944 HMI Reports ED 156

More recent HMI reports are in ED 156. One for Bebington C of E school of an inspection carried out on 1-2 November 1951 is in ED 156/5 (*see 10.5.6*).

3.14.12 School Digest Files ED 161

The Digest File for Bebington C of E Primary School (ED 161/1602) contains another copy of the HMI's report of 1-2 November 1951 and correspondence about maintenance work to be carried out in 1953 and 1960. Inside the back cover of the file is an accommodation schedule dated 22.4.1910 with the school number 169 crossed out and replaced by 34A.

3.15   List of Classes

3.15.1   Institution Files

3.15.1.1 Elementary Schools

1.   Chancery Close Rolls 1204-1903 (C 54)
      -       from 1725 private conveyances of land in trust for schools enrolled
              on dorse (back)

2.   Supreme Court Enrolment Books 1903-1992 (J 18)
      -       continuation of enrolment in C 54, include deeds conveying land
              in trust under School Sites Acts 1841 to 1852

3.   Legal Branch: Enrolled Deeds 1903-1920 (ED 191)
      -       four volumes of deeds enrolled under Mortmain and Charitable
              Trusts Acts 1888-1892 and Technical and Industrial Institutions
              Act 1892; mostly for public elementary schools

4.   Building Grant Applications 1833-1881 (ED 103)
-   application for grants towards cost of erecting public elementary schools

5.   Treasury Board Papers 1557-1920 (T 1)
-   contain similar applications and correspondence with PC Committee on Education on school building grants 1833-1902

6.   Sealed Plans and Drawings 1843-1872 (ED 228)
-   some of the coloured plans and elevations of school buildings accompanying building grant applications

7.   Elementary Education: Parish Files 1872-1904 (ED 2)
-   educational census returns and reports from schools outside London and boroughs, c1871; accommodation; school boards; new schools; examination schedules; loan sanctions

8.   Elementary Education: London Educational Returns 1871 (ED 3)
-   educational census returns for London; types of school; pupil numbers; classrooms; school income; religious connection; examination schedules; inspectors' reports

9.   Elementary Education: Local Education Authority Supply Files 1870-1945 (ED 16)
-   including educational returns for boroughs and other urban areas, c1871; accommodation

10.   Public Elementary School Files 1857-1946 (ED 21)
-   educational census returns for single-school parishes, c1871; accommodation; premises; organization; staffing; trusts and endowments

11.   Public Elementary Schools: Preliminary Statements 1846-1924 (ED 7)
-   tenure and foundation; accounts; accommodation; staffing

12.   Elementary Education: London Transfer Files 1871-1901 (ED 4)
-   tenure and foundation; accommodation; premises; government; trusts

13.   Primary Education: Schools Digest Files 1854-1984 (ED 161)
-   similar to School Files (ED 21), but with only main papers preserved

14.   School History Sheets 1870-1983 (ED 185)
-   size; status; location; sex and age range of pupils; building projects

3.15.1.2 Institution Schools

1.   Elementary Education: Institution School Files 1873-1945 (ED 30)
      -       schools in orphanages and institutions; accommodation; premises;
              organization; staffing

2.   School Districts 1848-1910 (MH 27)
      -       accommodation; staffing; building loans; auditors' statements;
              inspectors' reports

3.   Elementary Education: Poor Law School Files 1904-1953 (ED 132)
      -       selected poor law schools; inspectors' reports

3.15.1.3 Independent Schools

1.   Privy Council: Unbound Papers 1481-1946 (PC 1)
      -       including papers on school charters, statutes and endowments

2.   Independent and Private Schools: Returns of Private Schools not
      recognized for Grant or Efficiency 1919-1944 (ED 15)
      -       returns under the Education Act 1918 s 28 and the Education Act
              1921 s 155 with brief descriptions of art, commercial and vocational
              institutions; lists of private schools

3.   Certified Efficient Independent and Private Schools 1871-1944 (ED 33)
      -       applications for recognition as efficient mainly from charity and
              denominational schools, orphanages and, after 1927, profit making
              establishments, secondary schools and training colleges inspectors'
              reports

3.15.2   Endowment Files

1.   Elementary Education: Endowment Files 1853-1945 (ED 49)
      -       administration of endowments; schemes and orders

3.15.3   Local Authority Files

1.   School Districts 1848-1910 (MH 27)
      -       accommodation; staffing; building loans; auditors' statements;
              inspectors' reports; London school board expenditure

2.   Elementary Education: School Attendance Committee Files 1877-1902
      (ED 6)
      -       union school attendance committees (outside boroughs and school
              board districts); bye-laws

3.   School Board Office and Pupil Teacher Centre Files 1884-1911 (ED 57)
     -     mainly relating to the formation of centres providing secondary
           education for pupil teachers outside their own schools

4.   Elementary Education: Extra-District Children: Local Education
     Authority Files 1904-1945 (ED 89)
     -     approval of agreements between authorities; reports of public
           inquiries; disputes

5.   General Education: Local Education Authority Files: Establishment of
     Education Committees 1902-1966 (ED 139)
     -     schemes for constitution of committees

6.   Reorganization of Schools, Local Education Authority Files 1909-1945
     (ED 97)
     -     schemes and programmes for advanced elementary education from
           1925; returns to questionnaires; accommodation; central schools
           in London 1909-1910

7.   Education Acts 1918 and 1921: Local Education Authority Scheme Files
     1917-1932 (ED 120)
     -     development schemes for progressive education; schemes for
           compulsory attendance at day continuation schools

8.   Local Education Authority Grant Scrutinies Files 1920-1933 (ED 88)
     -     claims for annual grants to authorities; precedent files; grants to
           authorities; precedent files; reports to Parliament; inspectors'
           reports

9.   ' 1944 Education Act : Schemes for Divisional Administration 1944-1966
     (ED 151)
     -     objections to divisional administration schemes; claims for
           consideration as excepted districts (selected)

10. 1944 Education Act : Primary and Secondary Schools: Development
     Plans 1945-1966 (ED 152)
     -     plans; discussion of proposals; protests; proposals for provision
           for children with special educational needs

11. War of 1939-1945 Miscellaneous General Local Education Authority
     Files 1939-1959 (ED 134)

3.15.4   General Policy Files

1.   General Education, General Files 1865-1945 (ED 10)
     -     administration of educational legislation

2.   Elementary Education, General Files 1848-1945 (ED 11)
        -       policy; procedure; organization

3.   Schemes under 1918 and 1921 Acts, General Files 1918-1943 (ED 13)
        -       LEA schemes; committee reports; memoranda; circulars;
                parliamentary answers; statistics

4.   Elementary Education, London General Files 1870-1923 (ED 14)
        -       implementation of 1870 Education Act and later legislation

5.   Private Office Papers 1851-1935 (ED 24)
        -       confidential minutes, memoranda and correspondence; draft bills
                departmental committee reports

6.   Private Office: Files and Papers (Series II) 1935-1966 (ED 136)
        -       similar to ED 24; committee papers; working papers

7.   Central Advisory Council for Education 1945-1967 (ED 146)
        -       minutes, memoranda, correspondence, evidence and reports,
                published and unpublished

THE SPREAD OF EDUCATION.

"COME AND HAVE A LOOK, MARIER. THEY'VE BEEN AND PUT A
CHICK ON A LIDY'S 'AT, AND THEY DON'T KNOW 'OW TO SPELL
IT!"

Figure 8
'The Spread of Education' (*Punch*, December 3, 1902)

4.   SECONDARY EDUCATION

4.1   Central government involvement in secondary education

The nineteenth century saw a variety of secondary provision. Public schools, endowed grammar schools, higher grade schools, private and proprietary schools were all able to offer schooling beyond elementary level. Such state control as existed by the turn of the century was diversified: the Charity Commissioners for endowed schools; the Education Department, for higher grade schools and which supported some evening classes and day continuation schools; and the Science and Art Department, which administered grants to technical schools and science and art classes (*see chapter 5.1*).

4.2   Royal Commissions

4.2.1   Clarendon Commission

Dissatisfaction with secondary education increased as the nineteenth century progressed. Private initiative, for example by Dr Arnold of Rugby and followed by other public schools, led to changes. Official investigations also took place. Between 1861 and 1864 a Royal Commission on the Public Schools (Clarendon Commission) investigated nine such schools: Winchester, Eton, Westminster, Charterhouse, Harrow, Rugby, Shrewsbury, St Paul's and Merchant Taylors'. The schools were not very welcoming to the commissioners and they collected most of their information from questionnaires to headmasters and interviews with witnesses with special knowledge of public schools. The subsequent Public Schools Act 1868 resulted in more representative governing bodies and eventually in a more flexible curriculum. HO 73 contains the surviving papers of the commission; its report was published for Parliament (HC 1864 xx, xxi).

4.2.2   Taunton Commission

Some reforms were introduced, such as the Grammar Schools Act 1840, which freed the curriculum from exclusively classical studies, although many schools were introducing a wider curriculum. The endowed secondary schools and some private and proprietary schools were examined by the Schools Inquiry Commission (Taunton), which sat from 1864 to 1868. The assistant commissioners were both able and thorough; they included J G Fitch and James Bryce (who would later chair the 1894-1895 Royal Commission into the provision of secondary education). Matthew Arnold, son of Thomas, investigated secondary education in France, Germany, Switzerland and Italy; the Rev James Fraser looked into conditions in the United States and Canada;

authorities to provide municipal or county secondary schools or to assume responsibility for endowed ones. These earlier files also include Science and Art Department papers and records relating to pupil teacher centres where the secondary school developed from such establishments.

The second part of the class (pieces 3456-7149) are subject files created for each school in 1922, using the same official school number. They reflect the increased school provision after the First World War. The files also show the disappointment of progressive authorities both at the economies imposed on them by the recommendations of the Geddes Committee in 1921 and at the curtailed expansion plans brought about by the economic crisis ten years later. Further material on the work of the Geddes Committee is in ED 24/1301-11.

EXAMPLE:

ED 35/2442   1901-1921   Sutton County School for Boys (Surrey)
ED 35/6119-6120 1925-1942   Sutton County School for Boys

ED 27 contains files on endowed schools (papers between 1903 and 1921 are on ED 35 files), with estate management papers in ED 43.

EXAMPLE:

ED 27/2417-2434 1856-1900   Wyggeston Grammar School (Leicester)

ED 43/534   1910-1911   Wyggeston Grammar School Foundation

The main series of LEA files on secondary education is ED 53. Under the provisions of the Education Acts 1918 and 1921 an attempt was made to take a census of private schools: the surviving returns are in ED 15.

4.4   Free Places and Special Places

Although parents were given the right to free elementary schooling for their children in 1891, fee-paying secondary education persisted. Section 23(2) of the Education Act 1902 permitted LEAs to provide scholarships and pay fees. The Education (Administrative Provisions) Act 1907 introduced the free place scholarship system to give promising children from elementary schools the opportunity of admission to secondary school. Grant-aided secondary schools were permitted to admit free place scholars (not less than 25 per cent of the previous year's total intake) who had spent at least two years at public elementary school, in return for receiving a higher level of grant. Initially, the school received £5 per head for each scholar (ED 12/125, 327;

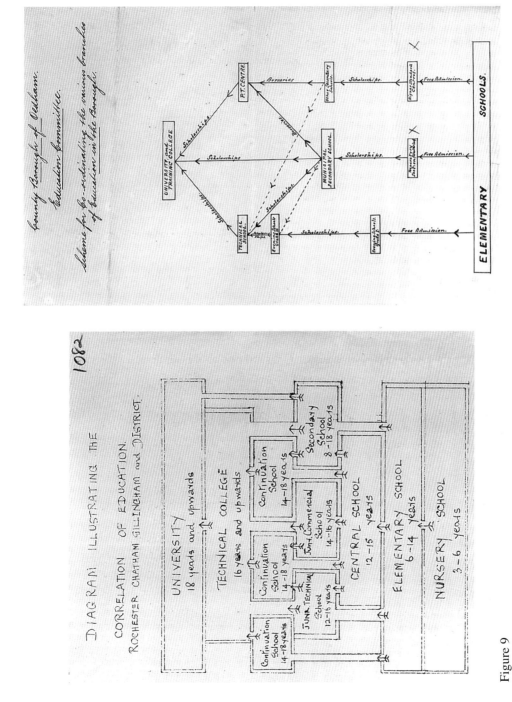

Figure 9

Left: evidence to Hadow report - diagram illustrating the correlation of education in Rochester, Chatham, Gillingham and district, 1926 (ED 10/147). Right: diagram of education in Oldham, 1904-1907 (ED 53/421)

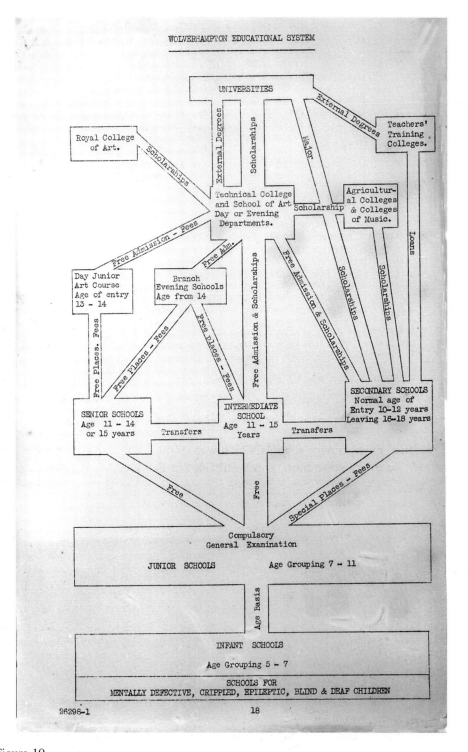

Figure 10
Evidence to Spens report - diagram showing proposed inter-relationships of educational institutions in Wolverhampton, 1930s (ED 10/151)

ED 24 code 48/3), although this figure was revised on several later o
1932 economy campaign caused free places to be converted into sp
which a means tested scale of fees was introduced (ED 12/354-367)
maintained secondary schools were abolished under the Education

General policy papers on fees and special places are in ED 12. Local authority ...
on free places for the period 1907-1921 are in ED 53, with some later papers in ED
110. ED 107 and ED 63 contain files relating to the award of maintenance grant by
LEAs. Not all authorities awarded maintenance grants, hence some gaps in the files.
Information on the administration of the special place system is in ED 55. (*See also
chapter 11.5.*)

4.5   Consultative Committee Reports

The Consultative Committee established by the Board of Education Act 1899 was a
mere shadow of the Education Council envisaged by the Bryce Commission; it could
only deal with matters referred to it and could not initiate any investigations. Despite
its limitations the Consultative Committee produced a number of forward-thinking
reports in the inter-war period. These reports are often known by the name of the
chairman: one was Sir Henry Hadow and another Sir Will Spens. The Hadow report,
Education and the Adolescent, was published in 1926 and mainly dealt with the
elementary sector which most children attended until they completed their schooling
at the age of fourteen. The Report recommended that primary schooling should end at
eleven and that pupils should then transfer to the academic secondary schools or to
more practical post-primary schools which were to be set up; if the latter did not
prove possible in the short term, pupils suitable for this kind of education would
transfer to senior classes set up to meet their particular needs. (ED 10/147, ED 24/
1265). Selection should be by examination (*see also chapter 11*).

The Spens Report of 1938, built on the work of the Hadow Report; where the latter
had put an emphasis on the potential of the modern school, Spens advised on the
other types of school as well. The *Report of the Consultative Committee of the
Board of Education on Secondary Education with Special Reference to Grammar
Schools and Technical High Schools* recommended parity of all types of school in
the state secondary system, with a tripartite arrangement of grammar, modern and
technical school (papers ED 10/151-153, 221-222; ED 12/530; ED 136/131).

4.6   Education Act 1944 (Butler Act)

The Hadow and Spens reports, the work of the Norwood Committee on examinations
(*see chapter 11.6*) and most significantly the effects of the war itself caused a
fundamental shake-up in educational thinking. The national system of education

suffered greatly during the war and a determination grew among parties interested in education that changes had to be made.

In June 1941 a memorandum was issued known as the 'Green Book'. It was intended to serve as a basis for discussion among all interested parties. The considerable response to this document and the 'summary' of subjects for discussion put out by R A Butler, the President of the Board, enabled a genuine debate and consultative exercise to take place on post-war education (ED 136/212-301).

The result of these extensive deliberations was the Education Act 1944, the Butler Act (Bill Papers ED 31/500-548; Private Office Papers ED 136/377-541). Its recommendations encompassed those of the Bryce Commission (*4.2.4*) on central administration, introducing a Minister of Education and replacing the Consultative Committee with an Advisory Council (papers in ED 146). Secondary education was redefined and reorganized. LEAs had to submit development plans covering both primary and secondary education; ED 152 contains those submissions.

ED 152 contains four types of file:

P/S LEA DP	-	Submission of development plan Discussion of proposals for primary and secondary schools Ministerial approval
P/S LEA DP(P)	-	Protests against the plan
M LEA DP	-	Special schools and special educational treatment
P/S LEA G	-	Supply (accommodation)

EXAMPLE:

Norfolk (a particularly well-documented county):

   P/S 429 DP - ED 152/116,469-475

These files contain area plans covering the whole county, including maps and detailed information about each school.

   P/S 429 DP(P) - ED 152/117

The protests file (*see 3.13*). It includes a tabulated summary of managers' and diocesan objections, arranged by area, with the LEA's comments.

M 429 DP   -   ED 152/118

Special schools and special needs file. This contains the Norfolk development plan, part III of which is a survey of special educational treatment and special requirements in the county. The other papers include a table of the expected numbers of children with special needs, divided into eleven categories.

P/S 429 G   -   ED 152/115

The supply (accommodation) file. This has been weeded. Surviving papers include tabulated details of the costs of various building options.

Public education was to be organized in three progressive stages: primary; secondary (representative digest files in ED 162 are a continuation of those in ED 35); and further (*see chapter 5*). Some papers on LEA schemes for their areas will be found in ED 53. The arrangements in Oldham, illustrated in diagrammatic form, serve as an example of the starting point there (ED 53/421).

General aspects of both primary and secondary education are covered in the General Files (ED 147); earlier files will be found in ED 10, ED 11 and ED 12. The file series in this class are as follows:

P/S LEA A	Attendance
P/S LEA B	Regulations
P/S LEA P	Extra district children
P/S LEA S	Miscellaneous
P/S LEA T	Religious instruction
G LEA G	Section 53 of 1944 Education Act, the provision of facilities for social and physical training
G LEA P(2)	Transport
G LEA Q	Provision of clothing

Further files in the S series are in ED 207.

4.7　Fleming Committee

In 1942 R A Butler appointed a committee, under Lord Fleming:

> to consider means whereby the association between the Public
> Schools ... and the general education system of the country could
> be developed and extended

The committee, in its report on *The Public Schools and the General Educational System*, suggested two ways in which this might be done. Scheme A, to apply mainly to day schools mostly 'direct grant schools' (those 250 grant-aided schools which chose in 1919 to be funded directly from central government rather than from LEAs), would abolish fees or grade them on a scale related to parental income; would allow LEAs to reserve a negotiated number of places for which they and parents would pay fees. Scheme B was for larger public boarding schools where LEAs would reserve 25 per cent of places for admission from maintained primary schools and the Board of Education would award bursaries to state sector pupils. Places would be recommended via a Central Advisory Committee.

The recommendations were a compromise and much criticized and the results were disappointing. The Central Advisory Committee was set up in 1947 but most places at independent schools were directly negotiated by LEAs and the committee was wound up in 1951. Papers relating to the work of the Fleming Committee are in ED 136/597-607, 667 and ED 12/518. ED 136/607 contains a copy of the report and ED 136/667 the report of the committee appointed to consider Fleming's recommendations in detail.

4.8　Central Advisory Council for Education

In 1945, under the terms of the Butler Act, the Consultative Committee was replaced by the Central Advisory Council for Education. The purpose of the council was to conduct investigations and to advise the minister on general education matters (ED 136/592-593). Its early reports and papers are also in ED 136: *Schools and Life* 1947 (ED 136/737); education and the young worker 1948, not issued as a report (ED 136/778); the relation between school and university 1951-1953 (ED 136/739-740); reducing compulsory school attendance 1952 (ED 136/742); and a report on early leaving 1954 (ED 136/743).

Later working papers, correspondence and evidence of the advisory council are in ED 146; two of those reports are of particular relevance to secondary education. In 1956 the council, under the chairmanship of Sir Geoffrey Crowther, was asked to investigate the education of boys and girls from fifteen to eighteen (ED 146/29-44). Its findings, entitled *15 to 18* but generally known as the *Crowther Report*, were published in 1959 and 1960. The main recommendations were raising the school leaving age to sixteen and the establishment of county colleges. In 1963 the council published its report on the education of average or less than average ability pupils between thirteen and sixteen (ED 146/45-63) called *Half our Future*, usually referred to as the *Newsom Report*. It repeated the call to raise the school leaving age and advocated a broader curriculum for these pupils, including practical work.

4.9   Comprehensive reorganization

In 1965, by the circular 10/65, all LEAs were asked to submit plans for comprehensive reorganization; a variety of possible options was offered. By 1970 most LEAs had either implemented schemes or produced plans. Although circular 10/65 was revoked by 10/70, this only slowed down the process of change. Papers on comprehensive education policy are in ED 147/825-831, 1282-1322.

A consultative committee was set up in 1965 to research the subject, following the recommendations of a Working Group. Only the minutes of the first meeting of the working group have survived (ED 209/1). The agenda, minutes and stage I of the report of the consultative committee are in ED 209/2-7. Parts II and III of its report are wanting. Other general papers of the committee are in ED 147/828-831.

A Public Schools Commission was set up in 1966, under Sir John Newsom 'to advise on the best way of integrating the public schools with the state system of education'. The following year an addendum was added to these terms of reference:

> To advise on the most effective method or methods by which the direct grant grammar schools in England and Wales and the grant-aided schools in Scotland can participate in the movement towards comprehensive reorganisation, and to review the principle of central government grant to these schools.

The first report on boarding schools was presented to the Secretary of State in April 1968 and published in two volumes. The Commission was immediately reconstituted under Professor David Donnison to consider those independent schools not covered in the first report. The second report was published in 1970. Minutes and papers relating to both reports are available in ED 148.

4.10   Case Study for Secondary Schools

The following table shows the main classes where records for the varying types of secondary school may be found; it is not exhaustive. This case study gives examples from the files on the first school in the table: Kendrick Girls' School, Reading.

Documents	Kendrick Girls' School, Reading, Berkshire (founded through work of Endowed Schools Commission)	Rutlish County Grammar School, Merton, Surrey (former endowed school taken over by LEA)	Mitcham County Grammar School, Surrey (LEA grammer school founded after 1902 act)	Sutton High School, Surrey (independent GPDST school)
Endowment Files (3 series by date)	ED27/77-92a ED 27/6832-6833 ED 27/9286	ED 27/4626-4635 ED 27/8539-8542 ED 27/9713	none	ED 27/8549
Endowment Estate Management Files (1 series)	ED 43/31-32	ED 43/934-935 none		
Post-Hadow reorganiz-ation (2 series by date)	ED 97/646 ED 97/761	ED 97/454 ED 97/761	ED 97/454 ED 97/761	ED 97/454
Develop-ment Plans	ED 152/360	ED 152/157-161	ED 152/157-161 161	ED 152/157-
Inspectors' Reports (5 series; 2-5 grouped in blocks of years geog-raphically by LEA)	ED 109/126-130 ED 109/8629 ED 109/9572	ED 109/5801-5806 ED 109/9122	ED 109/5811-13 ED 109/9347	ED 109/5872-5877 ED 109/9126 ED 109/9508
Digest Files	ED 162/138	page closed	page closed schools not covered	independent

4.10.1 Endowment Files ED 27

Kendrick School was founded with an endowment from John Kendrick in 1624. The endowment files for Reading School (ED 27/77-92a covering the years 1857-1896) include papers on the establishment of Kendrick Girls' School. One objective of the Endowed Schools Commissioners was to found grammar schools for girls from funds previously used exclusively for boys' education. Kendrick Girls' School was one of these. ED 27/85 contains a copy of the scheme for the school, approved 28 June 1875.

The second series of endowment files for Kendrick (ED 27/6832-6833) contain details of the administrative arrangements made to sell the Watlington House site to a Preservation Fund for £1705 plus auction expenses. In 1929 the Board approved a scheme for scholarships out of the endowment funds derived from the sale.

> The Governors believe that it will then be possible to reward
> conspicuous merit and to encourage deserving students more
> effectively than at present.

ED 27/9286 contains papers applying for further amendment of the Charitable Trusts Act (CTA) scheme of 1929 to allow greater flexibility in the award of scholarships. The Governors wished to channel the funds into helping those needing financial assistance, resident in the County Borough of Reading, with a preference for girls coming from public elementary schools. The scheme was altered in this way on 22 May 1936.

4.10.2 Estate Management Files ED 43

ED 43/31 contains papers for the years 1903-1909 including a report recommending the sale of three cottages forming part of the endowment of the school and an order by the Board of Education permitting the governors of the foundation to sell the land. The only other estate management papers available relate to an enquiry held in 1915 into converting funds into war loan stock (ED 43/32).

4.10.3 Secondary School Files ED 35

The first secondary school file for Kendrick Girls' School (ED 35/76) begins in 1902 with an application from the school seeking recognition as a Secondary Girls' School under division B of the Board's regulations. The school had to complete a detailed Memorandum about its application covering its curriculum and timetable. The Board raised questions over the laboratory provision and the arrangements for housewifery. Kendrick was put on the 1904 list of schools recognized as efficient.

The file also contains a lengthy report of an inspection in December 1903 *(for further details see 4.10.6 below)*. There are three further minor reports for the years 1905, 1906 and 1907. They are all brief reports to reassure the Board that the school conforms to its regulations. The first was based on three visits made by the inspector during the year (in June, October and November). It contains the following confidential remarks for the inspectorate alone:

> I was informed by the Headmistress that 8 girls in the first year
> course have been entered as candidates for the Cambridge Local
> Preliminary Exam. I warned her that the probable consequence
> would be the loss of the entire grant.

A note on the back of the report confirms that the correct application had been made to enter candidates for these examinations.

The second minor report in 1906 notes a lack of corporate spirit in the school and comments on the poor accommodation and the need to improve the teaching of French. The third report in 1907 makes no general remarks about the school because a full inspection is imminent.

That second full inspection followed in 1908 and another in 1914 *(for further details see 4.10.6 below)*. Much of the rest of the file is taken up with papers relating to the need for more school accommodation. It contains an architect's report, particulars of sewer works, an estimate for furniture and fittings for the new school and a specification for the new building dated 1920. The LEA tried to persuade the Board to sanction the use of funds from the Unemployment Grants Committee so that work could start on the site. The Board turned the application down.

The next file (ED 35/77) starts with papers on a change to the Charitable Trusts Act scheme for the school. The LEA wanted to ensure the continuation of a kindergarten at Kendrick Girls' School which meant an amendment to the existing scheme dated 2 March 1909. This was done and the new scheme was sealed in May 1910.

There are two files relating to Kendrick Girls' School in the second series of institution files; they cover the years 1922 to 1941. The story of accommodation is taken up again in ED 35/3515. The decision had been taken for Reading Borough Council to appropriate Sidmouth House and grounds in exchange for Watlington House. The situation was complicated because the latter was vested in the council as trustees of the foundation. The 1910 CTA scheme was superseded by a scheme authorizing the sale of the Watlington Street property and providing for the application of the proceeds. The new building was finally occupied in 1927 and new rules for the government of the school were drawn up; it became an LEA school.

The other file in the second series begins with information on the remedying of defects noted in the inspection of 1934, ie in the accommodation for art and housecraft and the need for more toilets. The other main subject of correspondence is the problem of 'early leavers'. Reading was quoted as a 'black spot for poor salaries and difficult financial conditions'. Parents were not honouring school life agreements and were removing their daughters at fourteen.

4.10.4   Post-Hadow Reorganization ED 97

The file for Reading Borough Council covering the reorganization required of LEAs after the Hadow Report (ED 97/646) makes one mention of Kendrick when discussing the future arrangements for advanced instruction in the western area of the town:

> . . . no account is taken of children who may go to the Kendrick or Reading Schools or to the new secondary school for boys (if provided) either as free placers or fee payers.

4.10.5   Development Plans ED 152

The main file on the Reading Development Plan (ED 152/360) states that Kendrick Girls' School is a type C secondary grammar school taking pupils between twelve and eighteen with a three form entry. Future building plans between 1946 and 1956 include a gymnasium, practical rooms and caretaker accommodation and the provision of a new playing field.

4.10.6   Inspectors' Reports ED 109

There are five series of inspectors' reports in ED 109, arranged by date; no individual school will appear every time in every series. Reports on Kendrick Girls' School appear in three of them. The first series of reports are clearly listed and dated but subsequent series are gathered together in blocks of years by LEA and it is not possible to work out from the list the precise date of the report for any particular school. Confidential information for the use of the inspectorate alone was regularly recorded in square brackets in the reports on secondary schools. The remarks were not intended to be included in the final report.

Copies of the full inspections of 1903, 1908 and 1914 which occur on the school file (ED 35/76 *see 4.10.3 above*) are also available in ED 109/126, ED 109/127 and ED 109/128 respectively. The 1903 inspection is known variously in related files as a first inspection, a full inspection or a special inspection; it gives details of the 'class in life' from which the 127 girls are drawn:

P	Professional and Independent	12
M	Merchants, manufacturers, etc	14
R	Retail traders	32
F	Farmers	1
C	Commercial managers, etc	28
E	Elementary school masters	—
A	Artisans and labourers	6
N	Not stated	25

The fees are 3 guineas under 8 and £5 over 8, per annum. Under the foundation there was no provision for boarding but a few girls were taken as boarders and their fees were £27 per annum. Attention was drawn to the poor state of the buildings and to the need for better French teaching.

That second full inspection followed in 1908. The number of pupils had varied between 137 and 162 in the last five years; 109 of the current girls were resident in the borough; the average length of time in the school was three years. The governing body was the same as for Kendrick Boys' School under a scheme amended under the Charitable Trusts Acts on 4 November 1901 and due to be amended again in 1909 to separate the two schools. Confidential remarks in square brackets reveal 'local feeling in favour of retaining old name'. The new CTA scheme suggests changing the name to Reading Girls' School. In the opinion of the HMI 'the title Kendrick is distinctive'.

HMI comment favourably on the history teaching which encouraged girls to record contemporary history as 'home affairs and colonial affairs'. The school had no monitors or prefects but did have a flourishing Old Scholars Society. The report includes the following synopsis of findings:

Excellences	**Defects**
PREMISES AND EQUIPMENT	New buildings a pressing need. Present Laboratory not used. Reference Library required.
STAFF Assistant Mistresses as a whole well selected	Head Mistress not very good, should be a new appointment when new buildings are erected. Competent Modern Languages Mistress necessary. Kindergarten Mistress lacking in knowledge of Kindergarten method.
SUBJECTS OF TEACHING	Time for Science insufficient; Form 3S not observed. Music needs reorganization.

The school received another full inspection in 1914. It had ten boys on its roll then in the Kindergarten. The largest 'class in life' represented was retail proprietors (33 per cent of girls' fathers). The majority of girls attended Kendrick for between two and three years and left before they were fifteen. There were also discussions about the number of free places available and about fees.

The report contains the following remarks about the teaching hours of assistant mistresses:

> 3.   Observations as to evidence (if any) of overpressure, due to teaching, supervision in and out of school hours, time spent in correction of exercises etc.:

> When the time spent in correction of exercises, preparation of lessons, and supervision of games out of school is added to above, the total amount is sufficient to account for the absence of buoyancy so noticeable in those members of staff who have spent many years in the school

The covering letter from the Board asked the LEA to satisfy two conditions: proper housing, ie buildings, and adequate staffing.

A fourth full inspection took place between 31 October and 2 November 1923; a copy of this report is in ED 109/129. It drew attention to the lapse of the kindergarten department. The confidential remarks related to the Head Mistress:

> The lessons she gave in Mathematics . . . showed strong evidence of lack of nervous control - she was once or twice almost incoherent. . . . The governors would have liked us to give them grounds for dismissing her.

The accompanying report of the conference with the governing body also remarks on the 'temperament' of the Head Mistress.

ED 109/130 contains a copy of an HMI report of an inspection in June 1934. By this time Kendrick has 393 pupils, 74 per cent of whom came from public elementary schools. The accommodation problems had been solved but the difficulty of early leavers remained. At the beginning of the conference on the report with the governing body, when the Head Mistress was not present, the Regional Inspector commented that 'the Head Mistress had succeeded to a great extent in overcoming her natural shyness'.

By the time of the next report in May 1951 a new Head Mistress had been appointed, the school roll was up to 544 with three streams and four VIth forms. It had two flourishing libraries and the teacher pupil ratio was 1:15. The school was experimenting with teaching Latin and English as one subject during the first year, to help an understanding of English grammar (ED 109/8629).

The most recent report available is one for an inspection which took place in March 1961. By this time Miss Towne had retired to be replaced as Head Mistress by Joan Hinley Atkinson and the number of pupils had risen again, to 568. The Latin/English experiment continued. The HMI suggested that the history department should make use of local archive material for studying the history of Reading (ED 109/9572).

4.10.7. Digest Files ED 162

The school digest file (ED 162/138) includes a copy of the 1961 inspectors' report but begins in 1945 with the visit of an HMI to look at catering arrangements. She decided that there was an urgent case for a new canteen. The rest of the file records progress and costs of various building projects for new classrooms, two laboratories, an art room and an art and craft room.

4.11   List of Classes

4.11.1   Institution Files

4.11.1.1 Secondary Schools

1.   Elementary Education: Higher Elementary School Files 1896-1926 (ED 20)
   -    preliminary statements: syllabuses; timetables; staffing; accommodation; some inspection reports; endowment schemes; university exhibition endowment papers; establishment of science schools and classes and teacher training courses in schools; papers on free places; premises and finance

2.   Secondary Education: Institution Files 1896-1946 (ED 35)
   -    applications for recognition; inspectors' reports; endowment schemes; university exhibition endowment papers; establishment of science schools and classes and teacher training courses in schools; papers on free places; premises and finance

3.   Secondary Education: Schools Digest Files 1879-1984 (ED 162)
   -    similar to Secondary Institution Files (ED 35), but with only the main papers preserved.

4.11.1.2 Independent Schools

1.   Privy Council: Unbound Papers 1481-1946 (PC 1)
   -    including papers on school charters, statutes and endowments

2.   Independent and Private Schools: Returns of Private Schools not recognized for Grant or Efficiency 1919-1944 (ED 15)
   -    returns under the Education Act 1918 s28 and the Education Act 1921 s155 with brief descriptions of art, commercial and vocational institutions; lists of private schools and institutions

3.   Certified Efficient Independent and Private Schools 1871-1944 (ED 33)
-    applications for recognition as efficient mainly from denominational and secondary schools and training colleges; inspectors' reports

4.   Home Office: Various Commissions: Records and Correspondence 1786-1918 (HO 73)
-    including papers of the Public Schools Commission (Clarendon Commission) 1861-1864

4.11.2   Endowment Files

1.   Secondary Education Endowment Files 1850-1945 (ED 27)
-    administration of endowments; schemes and orders; charities; estates and   property

2.   Secondary Education: Endowment Estate Management Files 1894-1924 (ED 43)
-    management of estates, property and other assets

4.11.3   Local Authority Files

1.   Secondary Education: Local Education Authority Files 1869-1946 (ED 53)
-    higher grade elementary schools and post elementary institutions pre-1902: schemes under Education Act 1902; free places; schemes for teacher training; schemes under Education Acts 1918 and 1921; reorganization of secondary education under Education Act 1944

2.   Secondary Education: Local Education Authority Grant Files 1921-1934 (ED 59)
-    grant aid to non-provided schools and direct grant schools

3.   Aid to Pupils: Local Education Authority Files 1919-1955 (ED 63)
-    schemes of assistance; annual accounts

4.   Secondary Education: Fees and Special Places: Local Education Authority Files 1932-1946 (ED 110)
-    fees and special places schemes; inspectors' reports on free place examinations

5.   Elementary Education: Maintenance Allowances: Local Education Authority Files 1921-1944 (ED 107)
-    schemes; inspectors' reports on educational requirements; returns of expenditure

6.   1944 Education Act : Primary and Secondary Schools Development
       Plans 1945-1966 (ED 152)
       -      plans: discussions of proposals; protests; proposals for provision
              of children with special educational needs

4.11.4   General Policy Files

1.   General Education, General Files 1865-1945 (ED 10)
       -      administration of educational legislation

2.   Secondary Education, General Files 1878-1946 (ED 12)
       -      regulations for secondary schools; memoranda and reports on
              teaching specific subjects; external examination policy; grant-aid
              and maintenance; fees and special places

3.   Central Advisory Council for Education 1945-1967 (ED 146)
       -      minutes and memoranda, correspondence, evidence and reports

4.   Primary, Secondary and General Education: General Files 1908-1974
       (ED 147)
       -      comprehensive education; examinations; career guidance; papers
              of Secondary Schools Examination Council, Curriculum Study
              Group, and Schools Council for Curriculum and Examinations

5.   Schools I Branch: Registered Files (S Series) 1966-1970 (ED 207)
       -      continuation of ED 147

6.   Private Office Papers 1851-1935 (ED 24)
       -      confidential minutes, memoranda and correspondence; draft bills;
              departmental committee reports

7.   Private Office: Files and Papers (Series II) 1935-1966 (ED 136)
       -      similar to ED 24; committee papers; working papers

5. TECHNICAL AND FURTHER EDUCATION

5.1   Science and Art Department

The importance of technical education for Britain's industrial and commercial supremacy was recognized in 1836 when the Privy Council Committee on Trade (later Board of Trade) obtained a government grant of £1,500 for the establishment of the first normal school of design, ie for the teaching of art as applied to commerce and industry. There is a Treasury long bundle (collection of papers) on this school covering the years 1836-1840 (T 1/4332) which includes the proposal for its establishment, the request for the grant and details of what a school of design should be and how it should operate.   Other information about the establishment of the school will be found among the correspondence of the Board of Trade (eg BT 1/462/ 909,467/2327).   Minutes of the committee of management of the school, from its inception in 1836 until 1849, are also available at the Department for Education Information Bureau (December 1836 to October 1847) and in ED 9/2 (October 1847 to January 1849). ED 9/3 contains further minutes of Board of Trade business relating to the school from February 1851 to December 1852. The following Parliamentary Papers contain reports on the early years of the school:

> 1841 xiii
> 1843 xxix
> 1844 xxxi
> 1845 xxvii
> 1846 xxiv
> 1847 lxii

From 1841 onwards, grants were made to support provincial schools of design in important industrial centres. The grants were administered through the PC Committee on Trade and correspondence between that department and the seventeen schools established by 1852 is in BT 1 (eg Ireland: BT 1/464/674A, 471/759; Norwich: BT 1/473/2243).

The Great Exhibition of 1851 was felt by many at the time to demonstrate that other nations were ahead of Britain in applied science. This resulted, the following year, in the reorganization of the Normal School of Design into the Department of Practical Art (BT 1/488/144/52, BT 1/502/279, BT 1/502/327; ED 9/3). A science department was added in 1853 and it became the Science and Art Department of the Board of Trade. Three years later the new department transferred to the Education Department but acted very much as a separate entity (*see 2.2*).

The Science and Art Department became involved in discussions with the Treasury and the Commissioners for the Great Exhibition about the construction and contents of a permanent museum on the Kensington Gore site (T 1/5907B/26540; T 1/5967B/ 19552; T 1/6031A/193; T 1/6059A/5636). The department wanted objects to be seen as widely as possible:

> if articles belonging to the central museum were circulated among
> the Schools of Art, and publicly exhibited, the instruction given
> in the Schools would be aided; the formation of Local Museums
> encouraged; the funds of the Local Schools assisted and the public
> knowledge of taste generally improved
>
> T 1/5967B/19552

The Science and Art Department was responsible for administering grant-aid to science and art schools. Correspondence about the administration of these grants survives among the Treasury Board Papers (T1/6099A/19336; T 1/6163B/20633; T 1/6168A/ 21055; T 1/6202A/14798). This system of 'South Kensington grants' encouraged the teaching of science, initially through evening classes. Until 1865 art school staff were required, in order to earn government recognition, to teach elementary school children. Manuscript minutes of the meetings of the Science and Art Department between 1852 and 1865 and printed minute books of the South Kensington museum and its branch museum at Bethnal Green between 1865 and 1876, when they were discontinued, are in ED 28. The more important files relating to the Royal College of Art have a separate subject heading among the establishment files of the Education Department and cover the period 1852-1950. (ED 23/16-64,65A,162-190,375,465,541-561,604,792,794-800,937-947). ED 83 contains other art school files, with later material (post 1944), in ED 167. ED 29 contains the Building Grant Files; correspondence and papers relating to art and science buildings are in WORK 17, with plans in WORK 33 (*see chapter 12*).

5.2   Committees and Commissions

5.2.1   Select Committee on Scientific Instruction 1868

The inadequacy of current technical education was raised with the Taunton Commission (*see chapter 4.2.2*). One result of this disquiet was the establishment of a Parliamentary Select Committee on Scientific Instruction under Bernhard Samuelson. This committee found that the main difficulties were the deficiency of elementary and secondary education and the shortage of science teachers. It recommended a sound system of secondary education, better facilities for science and a new scheme for elementary education (HC 1867/8 xv).

5.2.2   Devonshire Commission 1870-1875

The work of the select committee led to enthusiasm for a technological university but resulted in the appointment of a Royal Commission on Scientific Instruction and the Advancement of Science. It examined the work of existing institutions giving scientific instruction and produced eight reports (HC 1871 xxiv; 1872 xxvi; 1873 xxviii; 1874 xxii, xxviii). In its second report it recommended: that science should be taught in elementary schools and colleges; that the Science and Art Department classes should be inspected more efficiently; and that grants for their buildings and equipment should be increased.

5.2.3   Samuelson Commission 1881-1884

Very few of the recommendations of the Devonshire Commission were taken up but in 1881 another royal commission this time on technical instruction was appointed, chaired by Bernhard Samuelson. Its purpose was to compare the provision in this country with technical education abroad. It called for a unified system of elementary and secondary schools as a basis for sound scientific and technical teaching. Its main recommendations were: drawing, metal work and woodwork to be encouraged in elementary schools; science classes to be more practical and to be run by school boards and local authorities; building grants to be increased; greater efficiency in science instruction in teacher training colleges; and the proportion of scientific content in the curriculum in endowed secondary schools to be increased (HC 1881 xxvi; HC 1884 xxix, xxx, xxxi).

5.2.4   Technical Instruction Committees

Some progress was made. In 1886, for example, the London School Board approached the City Guilds to finance technical classes on its premises and promoted some experimental provision of technical classes in schools in Hackney and Southwark (ED 14/39). However, further encouragement was necessary.

The investigative activity led in part to the Technical Instruction Act 1889, which permitted local authorities to levy rates to aid technical or manual instruction (bill papers HLG 29/28). The distribution of aid was controlled by technical instruction committees of the recently formed county or county borough councils. General oversight was provided by the Science and Art Department, which interpreted the act widely to include almost all subjects except classics and literature. The new councils began to provide technical instruction both by day and evening classes.

However, the real stimulus to aid technical instruction came from 'whisky money'. The Local Taxation (Customs and Excise) Act 1890 raised duty on beer and spirits for local authorities to assist technical education or to relieve the rates (bill papers HLG 29/31). In the first year counties and county boroughs received £743,000. The bulk of the papers relating to the provisions of this act has been destroyed; surviving files are in ED 46. Another piece of legislation, the Technical Instruction (Amendment) Act 1891, permitted local authorities to aid institutions outside their boundaries and to offer scholarships to local students attending colleges beyond their own area (bill papers HLG 29/37).

By 1891, therefore, the whole country was covered by counties and county boroughs empowered to help to fill in the gaps in post-elementary educational provision. The technical instruction committees, the agents of the local authorities and forerunners of the LEAs, went beyond technical education to aid many forms of secondary and higher education.

EXAMPLE:

Four county grammar schools were founded in Surrey with whisky money. Richmond County School was one (ED 35/2436 covers the years 1896-1916).

In Surrey, H. Macan, chief officer to the technical instruction committee, saw that:

> a good secondary education is not only a necessary supplement
> to, but the very basis of, a sound technical education in all its
> higher branches

Macan echoed the Bryce Commission which had declared technical and secondary education to be inseparable and was able to carry out his policy because of the broad interpretation placed upon technical education by the Science and Art Department.

5.2.5   Departmental Committee on Technological Education

After the formation of the Board of Education in 1899 (*chapter 2.3*), the Duke of Devonshire, the President, set up a departmental committee on the co-ordination of technological education. It was chaired by Sir William de W Abney and included among its members Philip Magnus, director and secretary of the City and Guilds Institute and Swire Smith, a woollen manufacturer who had done much to develop education in Keighley, Yorkshire. In its report (ED 24/36) it recommended that the Board of Education should be the central authority for technical education and should control evening and continuation schools, approve courses of three to six years, and should authorize inspection under the Board of Education Act 1899. The committee felt that the Board should recognize the City and Guilds examinations and that more government aid should be given to technical instruction.

5.3   Education Act 1902

By the end of the nineteenth century a variety of forms of continuative education was available, whether technical, part-time, adult or further education, provided by a variety of bodies. It included day-release, evening schools, mechanics institutes, schools of art, polytechnics, university extension lectures, tutorial classes and various forms of working men's colleges and courses. With the passing of the Education Act 1902, changes were made in the conditions governing the award of parliamentary grant to encourage the expansion of technical education. Technical and continuative education became associated as LEAs took over most of the evening continuation schools, whether previously run by school boards, technical instruction committees or private bodies. Codes of Regulations governing the recognition of various forms of continuative, technical and further education were issued by the Board of Education for grant purposes.

Payment of a special grant for practical instruction in domestic subjects was first authorized under the Code of Regulations for Elementary Schools in 1875 (*see 11.10.1*) and foreshadowed similar arrangements for other practical subjects. New provisions were introduced in 1906 awarding grants for each course of instruction. Papers relating to the provision of these courses in both elementary and secondary schools are in ED 70, with the complementary LEA series in ED 96.

5.4   Trade Schools and Vocational Education

The need for preliminary technical education for young persons in preparation for employment in particular trades had been accepted from the end of the nineteenth century. These 'trade schools', which provided courses for boys and girls for two or three years after leaving public elementary schools, were recognized by the Board of Education in 1913 with the promulgation of Regulations for Junior Technical Schools. These regulations were subsequently incorporated in the Regulations for Technical Schools, Schools of Art and other forms of provision for Further Education in 1914 and succeeding regulations until the Education Act 1944 established the schools as an integral part of secondary education. Files on these schools are in ED 98.

The provision of technical education by means of day or evening classes or part-time or full-time vocational courses was regarded, for the purposes of the Regulations for Technical Schools 1905 and subsequent Regulations for Further Education 1926, as constituting a 'school' (until the term was redefined by the 1944 Act). Files on the 111 such 'schools' which existed by 1912 are in ED 82. Some subsequently sought recognition as Junior Technical Schools (ED 98).

5.5 Technical Colleges

Higher technical education involving prolonged courses of study was encouraged by the provision of a fixed annual grant to technical institutions. The work and organization of those institutes, subsequently described as Technical Colleges (ie Colleges for Further Education as defined in the Regulations for Further Education 1926 and 1934), are reflected in the Technical College Files (ED 90). These papers also contain information on the Grouped Course Certificates, a scheme initiated in 1907-1908, and on applications for approval of national certificate courses, which replaced the earlier scheme after the First World War. ED 182 contains the records of Joint Committees which administered the National Certificate and National Diploma Courses until the 1980s (*see chapter 11*).

5.6 Evening Institutes

The merging of evening continuation and evening technical school provision after 1902 resulted in LEAs and other managing bodies providing, within the terms of the regulations, part-time and evening courses, including day continuation classes and courses at works schools and elsewhere in a variety of vocational, domestic, art and general subjects. The files on these Evening Institutes, as they became known after 1926, are in ED 41; few papers survive prior to 1918.

5.7 Day Continuation Schools

The Education Act 1918 (Fisher Act) and the Education Act 1921 provided for compulsory part-time attendance at Day Continuation Schools by school-leavers between the ages of fourteen and eighteen. The scheme only ever came into partial operation and attendance reverted to the voluntary system as practised before 1918. Information on the provision, organization and curriculum of the schools, together with correspondence and minutes on various local arrangements, is in the Day Continuation Schools Files (ED 75).

5.8 Tutorial Classes

Tutorial classes evolved from the fusion of interests of the Workers' Educational Association and the University of Oxford in a movement to expand facilities for adult liberal education. The classes were recognized by the Board of Education in Regulations 1908/9 and grant-aided. Papers relating to such recognition before 1924 have been destroyed; ED 73 contains the subsequent files, including material on university extension courses and lectures. Files on vacation courses, designed as short residential courses of one or two weeks' duration, provided by 'Responsible Bodies' and subject to the same regulations and conditions as tutorial classes, are in ED 76.

Part of this same university extension movement led to the establishment of residential facilities. The first such college to provide a one year course of liberal adult education was Ruskin College, Oxford, founded in 1899 to promote higher education among working men and women. Direct grants to those colleges began after the First World War, and were subsequently embodied in the Adult Education Regulations 1924 and Further Education Grant Regulations 1946. Surviving files are in ED 68, though few are extant prior to 1930. Policy files on adult education following the 1924 regulations are in ED 80.

5.9   Developments since 1944

Major changes occurred in the organization of technical education after the Second World War. As a result of the Butler Act, each LEA had to draw up proposals for further education. Junior technical schools, commercial schools and schools of art were sometimes integrated into the revised system of secondary education. At the further education level, ED 155 and ED 46 contain papers on local authority schemes for the establishment of county colleges.

5.9.1   Percy Committee

The need for greater collaboration between the universities and the local authorities was acknowledged by the Percy Committee on Higher Technological Education. The committee reported in 1945 (papers in ED 46/295-296), and called for some technical colleges to develop courses of university standard, in conjunction with particular industries. ED 165 contains policy files on the establishment of these colleges and their development and progress. The committee also recommended the establishment of regional advisory councils to co-ordinate technological studies, with an equivalent body at national level.

The National Advisory Council on Education for Industry and Commerce was established in June 1948, following the recommendations of the Percy Report. Its functions were to review the development of education in relation to industry and commerce and to advise the Minister of Education accordingly. Information about the setting up of the council is in ED 46/699-750, 1032-1033, 1075-1118. Its later minutes and papers will be found in ED 205.

5.9.2   Robbins Committee

Until 1956 colleges offering further education were organized on a three tier system of regional, area and local colleges, with titles varying according to local preference and tradition. The white paper of that year on technical education (Cmnd 9703) proposed a four tier system, adding colleges of advanced technology (CATs); circular 305/56 (ED 142/10) gave further details of how this regional rationalization would work. Files on local and regional colleges are in ED 168 (similar in content to ED 90) and ED 166 includes files of CATs.

In 1963, after the report of the Robbins Committee on Higher Education (papers in ED 46/941-949; ED 116, ED 117 and ED 118; HC 1962-3 xi-xiv) some colleges, already removed from LEA control and financed by direct grant, were upgraded to technological universities, with degree-awarding status (*see chapter 7*). Papers on the financial implications of the Robbins report are in ED 188/10-15; ED 46/1037-1040 contain information on the conversion of CATs into universities; other material on the work of the committee is in ED 46/941-949. Files on major direct grant colleges are in ED 166.

5.9.3   Henniker-Heaton Committee

This committee was appointed in 1962 under the chairmanship of Charles Henniker-Heaton to examine how to maximize the opportunities for young people under eighteen to be released from work to attend technical education courses (day release). Information on the establishment of the committee is in ED 46/1008-1010,1961-1964.   Its report was published in 1964 (ED 204/4). The main recommendations were: day release for a further 250,000 young people by encouraging co-operation between LEAs and local industry; the provision of additional teachers and buildings; emphasis on occupations needing knowledge and skills where courses already existed combined with development work on courses for young people lacking educational training in employment and not requiring vocational training. The Ministry of Education and the Ministry of Labour should provide the statistical information necessary for planning day release and employers should consider further education for all junior staff.

5.9.4   Russell Committee

Adult education was examined by this committee. It was set up in 1969 as the Committee on Adult Education under the chairmanship of Sir Lionel Russell and its terms of reference were very broad: to assess the need for and provision of non-vocational adult education; and to consider its administration and financing. The committee produced its report *Adult Education: A Plan for Development* in 1973, covering all aspects of adult education and encouraging the partnership between statutory and voluntary bodies (ED 175/25). Its recommendations included: LEAs to draw up proposals for adult education; development councils to co-ordinate planning across England and Wales; revision of the regulations governing adult education and the universities; retention of the direct grant principle; educational leave with the co-operation of the Trades Union Congress (TUC) and Confederation of British Industry (CBI); improved accommodation and equipment. Agendas, minutes and papers of the committee, as well as evidence submitted to it, are in ED 175.

5.9.5   Other records

ED 167 contains files on Major Art Establishments. Between 1958 and 1971 there was a National Advisory Council on Art Education, which advised the Minister of Education on all aspects of art education in FE establishments. One of its aims was to create greater co-operation between art schools and industry, thereby improving industrial designs. Material on the setting up of the council is in ED 46/843-854 and its minutes and papers are in ED 206.

Exceptionally, the papers of the National Training College of Domestic Subjects (ED 164) have been presented to the Public Record Office. The College was founded in 1873 to promote the dissemination of a knowledge of cookery, became a limited company in 1888, extended its range of domestic subjects in 1902 and closed through lack of funds in 1961 (*see also chapter 11.10*).

In 1959 and 1964 responsibilities for agricultural education were transferred to the Ministry of Education. ED 174 contains files on this provision, reregistered from the Ministry of Agriculture and Fisheries. They cover general policy matters, as well as specific farm institutes run by LEAs and independent agricultural colleges. Earlier papers are in MAF 33 and related files are in ED 46.

The Ministry of Education set up a Research and Planning Branch in 1961 to commission and support research projects throughout the country. Its files (ED 181) include information on the establishment of the National Council for Educational Technology. Registered policy files of the Department of Education and Science on higher and further education are in ED 212 and cover such subjects as accommodation, recognition of courses and vocational training. Between 1948 and 1967 redistribution of expenditure among local authorities was organized by the Local Education Authorities Advisory Committee on Inter-Authority Payments; its minutes and papers are in ED 100. The minutes and papers relating to financial matters after 1968, particularly teacher training and advanced further education, can be found in ED 198. In 1969 a two year study was undertaken to look at the link between the cost of education and its effectiveness for sixteen to nineteen year olds. The committee was wound up in 1971, when the study was complete, but it is not clear whether it ever produced a report; ED 208 contains its minutes and papers.

In 1962 the Minister of Education set up the National Committee for the Certificate in Office Studies. The committee had no formal terms of reference; its task was to draft detailed rules for the award of the certificate and to publish them with guidance notes. The course was introduced in 1963 and the committee remained in existence until 1975 approving syllabuses and monitoring progress. Papers relating to the early meetings of the committee are in ED 46/869-870, with later material in ED 200.

The Department of Economic Affairs suggested in 1968 that a group was needed to co-ordinate activity between production and education departments. This initiative resulted in the formation of a Subcommittee on Management Education, chaired by the DES and reporting to the Industrial Policy Official Committee. The minutes and papers of this subcommittee are in ED 201.

5.10   Case Study for Manchester

We can use Manchester as an example of one county borough to illustrate the range of material available about technical and further education there.

Class	Description and Year	Place
Technical Institutions and Classes		
ED 29 85	building grant files 1896-1897	Moss Side, St Margaret's School
ED 70/3425 -3493 eg 3427 3444 3445 3473 3475 3488	practical instruction centres 1915-1929 1909-1929 1906 1906-1920 1914-1919 1906	Ancoats, Bengal Street Chorlton upon Medlock, Cavendish Council Chorlton Street Cookery Centre Moston, Lily Lane Council Municipal Training School of Domestic Economy Training School of Domestic Economy
ED 90/77- 86, 381-382 77-82	technical school files 1921-1935	Manchester Municipal College of Technology

83-84	1921-1935	Manchester Municipal High School of Commerce
85-86	1921-1935	Municipal Technical College
381	1936-1944	Manchester College of Technology (formerly Manchester Municipal College of Technology)
382	1936-1941	ditto - premises file
ED 75	day continuation school files	
eg 22-24	1920-1947	Newton Heath
ED 82 eg	technical school files	
329	1938-1939	Chatham Women's Institute
330	1937-1940	Openshaw
ED 98	junior technical school files	
68-69	1924-1933	Newton Heath
70-71	1924-1935	Openshaw
72	1928-1934	Trade School of Dressmaking
233	1942-1943	Ancoats, Mill Street School of Building
Art Colleges and Classes		
ED 83	art schools	
185	1919-1935	Municipal School of Art
316	1937-1943	" " " "
ED 167 eg	major art establishments	
395-399	1945-1968	Manchester Regional College of Art

Further and Adult Education		
ED 41/153-182,618 eg	evening institutes	
153	1921-1926	Ancoats, Mill Street (formerly Juvenile Unemployment Centre)
158	1918-1925	Chorlton upon Medlock Cavendish Council
163	1918-1925	Gorton, St Francis Roman Catholic
173	1918-1925	Openshaw Lads' Club
179	1918-1925	Upper Jackson Street Council
618	1920-1932	Newton Heath Technical
ED 73	tutorial classes	
18	1927-1935	Manchester University, dept of extra mural studies
110	1951-1954	" " "
63	1956-1968	" " "
67	1936-1945	Manchester University Joint Committee
35	1927-1935	WEA NW District
84	1936-1944	" " "
123	1947-1955	" " "
ED 76	vacation courses	
14	1946-1955	Manchester University Extra Mural Dept
ED 168/1864 -1914 eg	major establishments	
1864-1867	1940-1968	College for Adult Education

1871-1874	1948-1972	College of Commerce
1877-1879	1947-1966	Hollings College for the Food and Fashion Industry
1882-1883	1951-1966	College of Building
1884-1892	1945-1957	Southall Street Nursery Training Centre

Endowments

ED 37	endowments	
85	1895-1902	Hugh Becconsall's Charity
504	1906-1907	" " "
505	1921-1922	" " "
991	1935-1936	" " "
86	1889-1890	Mynshull's Charity
508	1908-1909	" "
509	1921-1922	" "
87	1886-1889	Simpson Memorial Trust
993	1936-1940	" " "
88	1899	Swanston Scholarship at Royal Manchester College of Music
510	1908	" " "
994	1940	" " "
506	1917	Edward Wadsworth bequest
507	1929-1930	Hiles Memorial Fund
992	1935-1936	Heywood Prize Fund

ED 74	private institutions	
133	1948-1966	College of International Marine Radiographic Communications
134	1948-1968	Northern School of Music
135	1946-1966	Princess Christian College
136	1948-1957	Wireless Telegraph College
LEAs		
ED 51	LEA Files	
54	1931-1935	Manchester County Borough
195	1936-1944	" " "
391-392	1946-1955	" " "
ED 58	classes for unemployed adults	
57	1933-1934	Manchester County Borough
ED 155	schemes for further education	
92	1948-1964	Manchester

5.11   List of Classes

5.11.1   Institution Files

5.11.1.1 Technical Institutions and Classes

1.   Practical Instruction Centre Files 1906-1957 (ED 70)
  -    provision of courses in domestic economy, cookery, handicraft, etc
        in elementary and secondary schools; acquisition of land and
        buildings; inspectors' reports

2.   Day Continuation School Files 1919-1947 (ED 75)
     -   provision of schools; organization; curricula; part-time courses for
         young workers

3.   Technical School Files 1912-1947 (ED 82)
     -   provision of technical courses; inspectors' reports

4.   Technical College Files 1907-1951 (ED 90)
     -   approval of courses; inspectors' reports; syllabuses; prospectuses;
         premises

5.   Junior Technical School Files 1919-1946 (ED 98)
     -   applications for recognition; inspectors' reports

5.11.1.2 Art Colleges and Classes

1.   Board of Trade: In-letters and Files, General (BT 1)
     -   includes correspondence on schools of design and Department of
         Practical Art

2.   Art School Files 1897-1949 (ED 83)
     -   provision of schools and classes; inspectors' reports; acquisition of sites
         and buildings; classification of schools

3.   Major Art Establishments 1931-1974   (ED 167)
     -   premises; changes of title; supplies of materials; approval of courses

5.11.1.3 Further and Adult Education Institutions

1.   Evening Institute Files 1901-1954 (ED 41)
     -   provision of evening institutes, day continuation classes, evening
         courses and works schools; applications for recognition of
         institutions and courses; prospectuses and syllabuses; staffing;
         inspection reports; accounts; premises

2.   Day Continuation Schools Files 1919-1947 (ED 75)
     -   provision of day continuation schools and classes; organization;
         curricula; part-time courses for young workers

3.   Adult Education: Tutorial Classes Files 1921-1969 (ED 73)
     -   recognition of courses provided by universities and voluntary bodies

4.   Adult Education: Vacation Course Files 1928-1955 (ED 76)
     -   recognition of courses; grants; student particulars

5.   Further Education: Major Establishments 1923-1979 (ED 168)
        -   approval of institutions titles and courses; premises

6.   Further Education: National Colleges 1944-1970 (ED 165)
        -   schemes for the establishment of colleges

7.   Further Education: Major Direct Grant Establishments 1930-1967 (ED 166)
        -   organization; syllabuses; annual reports; premises; extra-grant applications; minutes of governing bodies

5.11.1.4 Independent Institutions

1.   Further Education: Private Education Institution Files 1915-1955 (ED 74)
        -   recognition of institutions as efficient

5.11.2 Endowment Files

1.   Further Education Endowment Files 1854-1944 (ED 37)
        -   administration of endowments; schemes and orders

5.11.3 Local Authority Files

5.11.3.1 General

1.   Education Acts 1918 and 1921: Scheme Files 1917-1932 (ED 120)
        -   development schemes for progressive education; schemes for compulsory attendance at day continuation schools

5.11.3.2 Technical Education

1.   Practical Instruction Files 1899-1944 (ED 96)
        -   establishment of centres; lists of premises; inspectors' reports; courses

5.11.3.3 Further and Adult Education

1.   Further Education Files 1920-1968 (ED 51)
        - local facilities; inspectors' reports; annual estimates

2.   Further Education: Fees and Scholarship Files 1931-1955 (ED 55)
        -   local schemes; inspectors' reports; annual accounts

3.   Schemes for Further Education 1946-1967 (ED 155)
    -    plans and schemes for county colleges and further education; department's observations on proposals, modifications and final approval

5.11.4   General Policy Files

1.   Further Education: Adult Education: General Files 1923-1969 (ED 80)
    -    provision of FE under AE regulations 1924; co-operation with voluntary bodies

2.   Higher and Further Education Branches: Registered Files 1965-1972 (ED 212)
    -    accommodation; recognition of college courses; vocational training

3.   Research and Planning: General Files 1958-1975 (ED 181)
    -    grant-aided and commissioned research; papers on National Council for Educational Technology; subjects include handicapped children, further education, audiovisual aids, educational television, computers to formulate school timetables

4.   Finance Branch: Pooling Committee: Minutes and Papers 1968-1971 (ED 198)
    -    redistribution of expenditure among local authorities

5.   16-19 Cost Effectiveness Study Steering Group: 1969-1971 (ED 208)
    -    agenda, minutes and papers

6.   Committee on the Development of Day Release (Henniker-Heaton Committee) 1962-1964 (ED 204)
    -    agenda, minutes and papers

7.   Committee on Adult Education (Russell Committee) 1969-1973 (ED 175)
    -    agenda, minutes and papers; subcommittee minutes and papers

8.   Joint Committees for Vocational Education 1922-1982 (ED 182)
    -    minutes and papers

9.   National Committee for the Award of the Certificate in Office Studies 1967-1975 (ED 200)
    -    agenda, minutes and papers

10. Subcommittee on Management Education 1968-1969 (ED 201)
     -   minutes and papers

11. National Advisory Council on Education for Industry and Commerce:
     Council and Committees 1963-1970 (ED 205)
     -   agenda, minutes and papers

12. National Advisory Council on Art Education 1964-1970 (ED 206)
     -   agenda, minutes and papers

HIGHER EDUCATION.

Mr. Punch. "THAT'S ALL VERY WELL, BUT IT'S TOO DULL. LET THEM HAVE A LITTLE SUNSHINE, OR THEY WILL NEVER FOLLOW YOU."

Figure 11
'Higher Education' (*Punch*, November 22, 1890)

6. WELSH EDUCATION

6.1 Introduction

The development of education in Wales differed from that in England: the English system was largely imposed from above whereas the Welsh one grew mainly from popular demand; further, there were teacher training colleges in Wales before there was a national system of elementary education and university colleges were established before secondary schools. However, Wales also provided a model for England in the area of intermediate education, ie between elementary and higher.

The report of the Education Commissioners in 1847 focused attention on Welsh education and it severely criticized Welsh culture. The Treasury Board Papers contain the appointment of the commissioners (R R W Lingen, H Vaughan Johnson and J C Symons) in September 1846 (T 1/5193/20462), their accounts for expenses (T 1/5314/27590) and the sanction for payment for a translation of their report into Welsh (T 1/5361/10258). A copy of the report is in ED 17/10 and was published as a Parliamentary Paper (HC 1847, xxvii part I.1; HC 1847 xxvii, part II.1; HC 1847 xxvii part II.339). The Welsh demanded separate educational treatment. Impetus was given to the cause by the Reform Act 1867 which led to the election of influential Welsh Liberal MPs.

6.2 Aberdare Committee

A response to the demand for special consideration for Welsh education came in 1880 when a departmental committee was formed, under Henry Austin Bruce, Lord Aberdare, to investigate Welsh secondary education and to survey the supply of intermediate and higher education. At this time secondary provision consisted of: twenty-seven grammar schools in Wales, mostly sited away from the urban areas created by recent industrial expansion; a scattering of endowed schools such as Christ's College, Brecon and Llandovery College; and three secondary schools for girls at Dolgellau, Denbigh and Llandaff. Higher education was served by St David's College at Lampeter, Aberystwyth University College and a few Nonconformist academies and denominational theological colleges.

The Aberdare Committee looked at the provision for intermediate education, the establishment of provincial colleges, degree-awarding universities in Wales and funding. Its report (papers ED 91/8; HC 1881 xxxiii) revealed a state of affairs in Wales similar to that found in England by the Taunton Commission (*see 4.2.2*). The Aberdare report recommended the introduction of a new system of intermediate schools and the establishment of two colleges of higher education. It stressed the need to establish a system of education which was 'in harmony with the distinctive peculiarities of the country'. The second recommendation was implemented quickly with the setting up of university colleges at Cardiff in 1883 and Bangor the following year, the granting of equal status to Aberystwyth in 1890 and the formation of those three colleges into the University of Wales in 1893. The foundation of a secondary school system took rather longer.

6.3   Welsh Intermediate Education Act 1889

A J Mundella introduced several bills on Welsh intermediate education into the House of Commons in the 1880s but all foundered on the problem of its administration. The Local Government Act 1888 suggested a possible solution: the new county councils could become LEAs. The Welsh Intermediate Education Act 1889 established a national system of intermediate non-denominational schools. During the passage of the bill, however, the administration of the new schools was remitted to local Joint Education Committees (JECs) for each county and county borough. Bill papers are in HLG 29/28 and information about the administration of the act for the period 1892 to 1930 is available in ED 23/605.

These committees had to submit schemes for secondary and technical education to the county councils and the Charity Commissioners. The Commissioners, who had the right to be represented at meetings of the JECs, in turn submitted schemes to the Education Department. They were also required to present an annual report to both Houses of Parliament on proceedings under the act which was taken as one with the Endowed Schools Acts. County councils could levy a °d rate for approved schemes which the Treasury would match with an equivalent grant on condition of an annual inspection of the schools.

Within six months of the act becoming law all sixteen JECs were in operation and in the years 1890 to 1892 they held ten conferences. W N Bruce, son of Lord Aberdare, was the Charity Commissioners' representative at these meetings. The first county scheme was established in Caernarvonshire in 1893 and the last in Glamorgan three years later. In seven years eighty-eight new schools were opened, with over sixty local government bodies and sixteen county governing bodies operating a county scheme. By 1903 there were ninety-five intermediate schools with 8,789 pupils.

EXAMPLE:

    Caernarvon:

| ED 35/3130 | 1901-1923 | Caernarvon Co School |
| ED 35/3131-3137 | 1900-1908 | Intermediate and Technical Education Fund |

Files on the individual schools are in ED 35. Since the Welsh Intermediate Education Act resulted in the local authority status of the majority of Welsh schools, there is less material on the Welsh files relating to property and domestic matters than on their English counterparts. However, papers peculiar to the Welsh files include those dealing with the private lodgings of children during term time and with the teaching of Welsh.

A J Mundella was pleased with his achievements in Wales. In 1893 he wrote to his friend John Viriamu Jones, Principal of University College Cardiff:

> I am well satisfied with the progress of education in Wales. My initiative is working like a little leaven, and I hope when Wales has worked out its own salvation, it will have the effect of leavening the larger and more inert mass of Englishmen. I always desired to see Wales become a model for our national system, and I am increasingly hopeful that it will gradually become so.

His wish was granted because the Welsh Intermediate Education Act did foreshadow events in England by providing a pattern for the control of secondary education by county councils.

6.4   Central Welsh Board

The Schools Inquiry Commission of the 1860s (*see 4.2.2*) first mooted the idea of a co-ordinating board for Wales. The Treasury required a body with local knowledge to supervize inspections and examinations in the intermediate schools; the Central Welsh Board (CWB) was established in 1896 to fulfil this role. The Charity Commissioners acted as a buffer between the CWB and the Treasury.

Records reflecting the work of the Central Welsh Board are in ED 35 and ED 27. Since both the Department (later Board) of Education, and the CWB reported on Welsh schools there are more inspection reports for those schools on the institution files than for their English equivalents. The ED 35 files also contain CWB and Intermediate and Technical Education Treasury Grant Files (ED 35/3406-3448). These include the annual reports submitted to the Charity Commission (and later to the Board of Education) for transmission to the Treasury (ED 35/3417-3428); domestic matters concerning the CWB; and discussions on Welsh education policy.

6.5   Balfour Act 1902

In Wales, many districts refused to operate the act because the Nonconformist inhabitants objected to the extension of rate aid to voluntary schools (ie Church of England schools). This opposition was so strong that a movement composed of 'passive resisters' was formed, led in Wales by Dr Clifford, a Nonconformist minister, and in the House of Commons by David Lloyd George. The passive resisters refused to pay the levy and suffered distraint upon their goods. Information on the resistance movement will be found among the Private Office Papers (ED 24/13a-34, 578), the Bill Papers (ED 31/22), the Welsh General Files (ED 92/1), and the Elementary Education, LEA, Miscellaneous Files (ED 111/258, 264, 266, 269).

A confidential memorandum on the defaulting authorities was prepared in June 1904 (ED 24/577). The situation was finally resolved by the Education (Local Authorities Default) Act 1904, which, during its passage through parliament, became known as the 'Coercion of Wales Bill'. It provided that, if an authority failed to make adequate grants to voluntary schools in its area, the Board of Education could deduct from the grant paid to it sufficient money for those voluntary schools; these sums would be paid direct to the relevant school managers. The bill papers are in HLG 29/84. After several years of animosity, the Balfour Act was eventually accepted in Wales.

6.6   Welsh Department of the Board of Education

The Welsh Nonconformist opposition to the Education Act 1902, together with the return of a Liberal government with strong Welsh support, led to the establishment of the Welsh Department of the Board of Education in 1907. The new department was responsible for all aspects of elementary and secondary education in Wales and later took on technical education, schools of art, further education and training colleges. Papers on the organization of the new department from 1908 up to 1927 are in ED 24/580 and ED 23/600. A separate inspectorate for Welsh schools was also set up in 1907.

The teaching of Welsh was a contentious issue in the Principality. As early as 1849 Kay-Shuttleworth had anticipated that the development of elementary and secondary education was a threat to the Welsh language when he instructed his Welsh inspector, the Rev H Longueville Jones, to promote a bilingual policy. The Cross Commission (*see 3.5*) recognized Welsh as a grant earning subject under the elementary code and Welsh was included as a class subject in elementary schools (ED 92/8). However, by the turn of the century little attention was being paid to the teaching of Welsh and the Central Welsh Board was dubbed the Central French Board because of its advocacy of that language.

The Welsh Department was able to change a 'bilingual difficulty' into a 'bilingual opportunity' by introducing the Welsh language into elementary and secondary schools and training colleges; teaching was bilingual where LEAs wanted it (ED 91/13 and 57). The new department also encouraged the construction of new council schools in areas with previously only one Church of England school, thus helping to damp down discontent over the voluntary school issue.

Questions about the interpretation and application of the 1902 Act continued to be raised. In the case of Oxford Street C of E school Swansea in 1911, the LEA asked the Board of Education whether it should spend an equal amount on a voluntary school as on a council one. The answer was equivocal and the LEA took the matter to court. The resulting decision, known as the Swansea Judgment, was that differentiation between school and school could be legally made but it must in all cases be justifiable. Papers relating to this judgment are in ED 11/12; ED 111/251; T 1/11202/8810/10, T 1/11293/10146/11; and to the particular school in ED 21/22722-22730.

The main papers of the Welsh Department relating to aspects of general, elementary and secondary education are in ED 91, ED 92 and ED 93 respectively. Reports on Welsh schools occur on the institution files and on these general files (ED 91-ED 93). ED 22 contains a separate series of inspectorate memoranda for the years 1907-1940; most of the later series of memoranda in ED 135 was also adopted in Wales.

There was conflict between the Welsh Department and the Central Welsh Board. The 1909 annual report of the Welsh Department (ED 24/588) put the disagreements into print:

> the Central Welsh Board should now consider to what extent their rigid examination system might be the cause of the wooden and unintelligent type of mind of which their examiners complained. Elasticity and adaptability of curricula, and the development of differentiation among schools were difficult under such a highly centralised system of examinations.

An attempt was made to settle these differences in 1918 by the appointment of a departmental committee, under the chairmanship of W N Bruce. It was to advise on how the organization of secondary education in Wales 'may be consolidated and co-ordinated with other branches of education, with a view to the establishment of a national system of public education in Wales'. One of the main recommendations of the committee, which reported in 1920 (HC 1920 xv), was a National Council for Education in Wales, replacing the CWB and the University Court. Committee papers and a copy of the report are available in ED 24/1185 and ED 23/118.

The post-1921 development of secondary education in Wales (following the Bruce recommendations) should be seen against a background of continuing difficulties between the Board of Education and the CWB. A few Central Welsh Intermediate Education Fund general files are extant (ED 35/7129-7134) and contain various proposals for a solution to these problems, such as a unified inspectorate, changes in the financial structure of the CWB, the establishment of a National Council for Education in Wales, and the transfer of the functions of the CWB to the University Court of Wales.

6.7   Butler Act 1944

Under the provisions of this act with the dissolution of the Consultative Committee, a separate Central Advisory Council for Wales was established. Its papers are in ED 136/594-596, 745-751, 879-888 and ED 46 and ED 146. They include a report on the future of secondary education in Wales (ED 136/749 and 751). Welsh development plans files under the 1944 act are in BD 7.

EXAMPLE:

BD 7 contains the development plans for Merthyr Tydfil for primary and secondary schools, approved by the local education committee 28th August 1947. It includes a map of the jurisdiction of the county borough of Merthyr marking:

> existing voluntary schools
> existing LEA schools to be closed
> new voluntary schools
> new LEA schools
> existing schools to be adapted

Each school is labelled by the following key:

N	nursery
I	infants
IJ	infants and junior
J	junior
Sn	senior
M	modern (secondary)
G	grammar
U	unreorganised
H	hospital

Powers over Welsh education have gradually been transferred to the Welsh Department since its inception. This movement has been more marked after the Butler Act. In 1956 an office was opened at Cardiff and in 1970 responsibility for most aspects of primary and secondary education in Wales went to the Welsh Office. Separate series of files for Welsh schools were raised. ED 216 contains some elementary school files but also material on primary and secondary schools, including policy information on the closure of rural Welsh-speaking schools. Policy matters post-1944 will usually be found on the Welsh Department General Files (ED 220). These include papers on the establishment of the Welsh Joint Education Committee. Many early files in this series were damaged by flooding at Cardiff in 1960.

6.8   Technical and Further Education

After 1889 technical education (*like intermediate education: see 6.3*) was administered by a local authority called the Joint Education Committee for each county or county borough. The system paved the way for the expansion of technical education in Wales. In 1889 the Cardiff Technical Instruction Committee was formed and links were forged with the university. Mining and metallurgic departments were also formed at Cardiff, with over 700 students. Night schools for young colliers flourished in Mid Glamorgan and Monmouth and by 1892 technical classes were established throughout South Wales. Three years later, Cardiff Technical School provided 50 different courses in science and art and had 2,600 students.

Some files on the administration of the grant for technical education are in ED 35/ 3436-3448. Information about Welsh technical education will generally be found on the same series of files as similar English education (*see chapter 5*). Responsibility for further education was transferred to the Welsh Office in 1978; more recent policy files and institution files are in ED 219.

6.9   Universities

The Welsh university movement was begun by Welsh clergy in England. St David's, Lampeter, founded in 1827, was the first college of higher education and did not merge with the University of Wales until 1967. Aberystwyth University College opened in 1872 (ED 119/68-69). However, there were few secondary schools to produce students for these establishments; in 1879 there were 189 Welsh students of higher education. The Aberdare Committee (*see 6.2*), reporting in 1881, recommended the establishment of provincial colleges and a degree awarding university in Wales. Two colleges were set up at Cardiff in 1883 (ED 91/14, ED 119/74-77) and Bangor the following year (ED 119/70-73). A meeting in Shrewsbury in 1891 decided that a teaching rather than merely an examining university should be the model, with the ability to confer degrees on its own students, who should have residential qualifications. The federal principle was also adopted and the three university colleges became constituent parts of the University of Wales in 1893.

Information about the Treasury grants to the University of Wales will be found in ED 24 Code 55/6 (ED 24/570-575, 2024-2029). The report and evidence to the committee on the University of Wales 1907-1909 are in ED 24/573. During the First World War a Royal Commission was set up on the same subject. This was the Haldane Commission 1916-1918 which recommended an overhaul of university administration and the establishment of another university college at Swansea. Its report is available (HC 1917-18 xii, xiv) and there are further papers in ED 24/2026-2027. The University Files (ED 119) contain further papers on the University of Wales in general for the period 1906-1944 (ED 119/81-84) and University College Swansea in particular (ED 119/78-80).

6.10   Teacher Training

Many Welsh teachers were trained at Borough Road training college. A few training colleges existed in Wales, eg Brecon Normal School briefly in 1846, and there were C of E training colleges at Trinity College Carmarthen (1848), Caernarvon (1849) and Bangor Normal College (1858). General information about training colleges, pupil teacher centres, teachers salaries, etc are in ED 91-ED 93. Institutional files are generally in the same classes as their English counterparts. The Welsh Office took over responsibility for teacher training from the DES in 1978 and more recent teacher training institution files are in ED 217. Similarly, later teachers' staffing files are in ED 218 (*see also chapter 9*).

6.11   List of Classes

This list itemizes only those classes which are specific to Wales. Generally, information about education in Wales will be found in the same classes as its English equivalent. Readers are therefore referred to the lists of classes for each subject area.

1.   Welsh General Education, General Files 1880-1938 (ED 91)
    -    Welsh Department annual reports; area reports; committee papers; teaching of Welsh; statistics

2.   Welsh Elementary Education, General Files 1885-1939 (ED 92)
    -    Welsh reaction to 1902 Act; office procedure; teaching of Welsh; curriculum; buildings; regulations; school camps; reorganization of rural schools

3.   Welsh Secondary Education, General Files 1900-1935 (ED 93)
    -    administrative arrangements; procedural instructions committee papers, regulations

4.   Welsh Department: General Files (W Series) 1944-1976 (ED 220)
    -    policy matters including establishment of Welsh Joint Education Committee

5.   Welsh Department: Registered Files (Various W Prefixes) 1893-1983 (ED 216)

6.   Welsh Department: Further Education (WT Series) Files 1945-1977 (ED 219)
    -    policy matters and institutions including farm institutes, colleges of technology, colleges of FE, outward bound schools, art colleges and independent FE institutes

7.   Welsh Department: Teacher Training Institutions Files (WR Series 1929-1969 (ED 217)
     -   gender ratio of students; teaching through Welsh; finance; expansion of premises

8.   Welsh Department: Special Schools Files (WM Series) 1904-1974 (ED 224)
     -   organization of residential and hospital schools

7. UNIVERSITIES

7.1 Introduction

Until the nineteenth century Oxford and Cambridge were the only universities in England and there were none before that in Wales. The public records contain some information about their administration from the medieval period onwards. The Exchequer, Various Accounts (E 101), for example, include accounts of the Warden of King's Hall, Cambridge, information about the expenses of scholars and some warrants and receipts for payment of annuities, etc by various Oxford and Cambridge colleges, from the reign of Edward II to that of Elizabeth I (E 101/348/1-40).   The Miscellaneous Books of the Exchequer Augmentations Office include surveys of the universities for 37 Henry VIII [1545-1546] (E 315/440-441).   The State Papers Domestic also contain numerous references to Oxford and Cambridge.

The records of the Privy Council and the Treasury are, however, the main sources of information for the nineteenth century. The former was responsible for providing advice about the suitability of university charters and statutes (PC 1 and PC 8), the latter was involved in any financial transactions between government and the universities (T 1). Both had an interest in any Royal Commissions which investigated university activities.

Little scope for change was possible within the rigid framework imposed by individual College statutes, most of which pre-dated 1600. Both universities remained the preserve of the Church of England, largely open only to those of the Anglican faith who could pay their own way and dominated by a very traditional curriculum, although closed scholarships, endowed by individual benefactors and open only to pupils from particular grammar schools attending certain colleges, provided limited access to higher education for some poorer students.

7.2 Royal Commissions

7.2.1 Oxford and Cambridge Commission 1850-1852

Some improvements had taken place at the two universities by the mid-nineteenth century but progress was not sufficiently swift. A petition was presented to Lord John Russell, the prime minister, urging him to ask the Queen to appoint a royal commission. The commissioners were comparatively well received at Cambridge but encountered great opposition at Oxford. Two reports were issued   (Oxford HC 1852 xxii; Cambridge 1852-3 xliv) which formed the basis of the Oxford University Act 1854 and the Cambridge University Act 1856. The aim of the legislation was to remove obstacles which hindered the development of the universities; there was to be no state interference.

The main provisions of the acts were to broaden the representation of the governing bodies (the Hebdomadal Board at Oxford and the Caput at Cambridge) and to enable discussions to take place in English rather than Latin. Other changes included: opening up closed scholarships and fellowships to competition; removing some religious tests; founding new professorships, augmenting the endowments of existing ones and giving professors more say in the administration; modifying the tutorial system; attempting to reduce the cost for students.

Further commissions were appointed in 1854 under the legislation to continue the work of reform. Papers relating to the work of these commissions are for Oxford in HO 73/37-49 and T 73/1 (HC 1857-8 xx) and for Cambridge in HO 73/64-68 (HC 1859 sess 2 xix).

7.2.2   Cleveland Commission 1872-1874

As a result of the reforms which followed the acts of 1854 and 1856 greater vigour was introduced into university life: the number of students increased, new studies were introduced, and many of the most obvious defects were corrected. New colleges such as Keble at Oxford and Selwyn at Cambridge were established to cater specifically for poorer students. The revival of the two universities was linked to the revival of the Church of England. However, it was felt that more could be done and a second royal commission on Oxford and Cambridge was appointed in 1872 under the Duke of Cleveland. Unusually, Cabinet papers survive about its establishment (CAB 41/3/46). It reported in 1874 (HC 1873 xxxvii) and three years later its recommendations resulted in the Oxford and Cambridge Act 1877. This act set up commissioners to reform the college statutes. Life fellowships were abolished, fellowships for research were instituted and fellowships with teaching duties and salaries were standardized. New professorships were established and endowments of existing chairs increased by annexing them to college fellowships.

7.2.3   Selborne Commission 1889

The dissatisfaction with the existing universities led to different developments in London. A college was founded in Gower Street in 1828 which was non-denominational, non-residential, charged low fees and taught modern studies and science. King's College, a similar institution but founded on Church of England principles, was established in 1831. Five years later the University of London was granted a charter and had the power to confer degrees and to affiliate other institutions; the Gower Street building was renamed University College.

The University of London was in the anomalous position of being able to award degrees on the basis of its examinations but not being a teaching body. It ceased to exercise its power to affiliate in 1858, by which time some of the affiliated establishments were no more than secondary schools. Proposals were made to set up a separate teaching university. The threatened secession led to the appointment of a royal commission under Lord Selborne in 1889.

The findings of the Selborne Commission (HC 1889 lxxxix) were not acceptable to University and King's Colleges. The two colleges decided to secede and form a new teaching university to be called Gresham University.

7.2.4   Gresham Commission 1892-1894

Further government intervention led to the establishment of the Gresham Commission in 1892. The commissioners came out against two universities for London (HC 1894 xxxiv) and after two abortive attempts the London University Commission Act was passed in 1898 and new statutes were put into operation in 1900. London University was given the greater part of the Imperial Institute in South Kensington as its administrative headquarters.

7.2.5   Haldane Commission 1909-1913

The reconstitution of the university at the end of the nineteenth century as a teaching and an examining body was an important stage in its development but it resulted in a complicated organization of diverse institutions which caused administrative problems. These difficulties were tackled by the Royal Commission on London University (Haldane Commission) appointed in 1909. It reported four years later recommending a faculty organization (HC 1913 xl). A departmental committee was set up to work out the implications of the Haldane recommendations. Various working papers of the committee are available: ED 23/99, 320; ED 24/1171, 1196, 2019-2022; UGC 5/1-2. War delayed implementation which was finally brought about by the University of London Act 1926 which provided a new constitution and appointed statutory commissioners to frame statutes in accordance with the departmental committee's recommendations. Bill papers are in ED 24/1106-1111, ED 31/251, T 161/180/S16608, T 163/30/4, with Cabinet Office Home Affairs Committee discussions in CAB 26/8; PC 10/50-80 and T 160/260/F10239 contain the papers of the Statutory Commission; the powers of the commissioners are defined in TS 27/311; and information on the statutes they recommended between 1927 and 1929 is in ED 24/2015.

7.3   Development of provincial universities

Various attempts were made to establish other universities. In February 1656, for example, the Privy Council issued an order to apply the sequestrated revenues from Durham cathedral for the establishment of a college (SP 18/124, no 20). Two years later the college petitioned Richard Cromwell to grant university status but the

Restoration intervened and the endowments were returned to the dean and chapter. The notion of a university at Durham was revived at the beginning of the nineteenth century. An act of 1832 permitted the dean and chapter to endow a university from the revenues of the see and the cathedral chapter; the charter was issued in 1836. A century later, Durham University was the subject of two inquiries into its constitution and government: one by Sir Amherst Selby Bigge 1926-1933, and the other a consequent royal commission 1933-1937; the surviving papers of both inquiries are in ED 112.

Owens College was established in Manchester in 1851 and ran courses for degrees from London University; from 1871 it was permitted to admit women. In 1880 the Victoria University was set up in the north of England with Owens College, Manchester as its first member institution. University College, Liverpool (founded in 1881) was affiliated to the Victoria University in 1884 and Yorkshire College, Leeds (founded in 1874) in 1887. The components of Victoria University separated in 1903 to form independent universities in each city. Some information on these mergers and later separations will be found in ED 119/50 (Manchester), ED 119/25 (Liverpool) and ED 119/20 (Leeds). ED 24/511 includes the reports of the committee of the Privy Council on the grant of charters to Liverpool and Manchester; PC 8/605 contains the grant.

Birmingham University evolved from a college founded by Josiah Mason in 1880 and was granted its own charter in 1900 (ED 119/1; PC 8/516). Others followed suit, eg Nottingham in 1948 (PC 8/582) and Bedford College for Women in 1926, under the terms of the University of London Act (PC 8/668).

7.4   Treasury Grants

The colleges could only obtain charters as independent universities when they could satisfy the Privy Council that their financial position was sufficiently sound for them to function properly as universities. Some had endowments, usually for scholarships and prizes, originally administered by the Charity Commission; surviving papers are in ED 39. A few institutions received aid from the Treasury: some Oxbridge colleges as compensation for loss of ancient vested rights or ancient charges on the land revenues; London colleges (for dissenters) and Queen's Colleges in Ireland (for Roman Catholics) when entrance elsewhere was barred by religious tests; Welsh colleges at Aberystwyth, Bangor and Cardiff to encourage higher education in Wales (*see 6.9*). Details of these early grants are in UGC 5/18.

In 1889 parliamentary grant was made available on application for the first time to university colleges in Great Britain

> to strengthen the position of selected poorer colleges and to stimulate local munificence.

The initial Treasury grant totalled £15,000. Twelve colleges made claims but only eleven were successful; Hartley Institution, Southampton was refused. ED 24/77 contains a copy of the House of Commons return of 1889 showing the payments:

Owens College Manchester	£1,800
University College London	£1,700
King's College London	£1,700
Liverpool University College	£1,500
Mason College Birmingham	£1,400
Yorkshire College Leeds	£1,400
Nottingham University College	£1,400
Bristol University college	£1,200
Durham College of Science at Newcastle	£1,200
Firth College Sheffield	£1,200
Dundee University College	£ 500

The grant was conditional: each institution had to make provision for postgraduate research. Information about these grants will be found in the university files (ED 119) and in the Treasury Board Papers (T 1) until 1918 when the Deposit Accounts Ledgers begin (T 252).

The general grant was administered by the Treasury on the advice of various ad hoc committees on grants to university colleges; reports of these committees are in T 1 and further papers for the years 1889-1910 in UGC 5/19-24. In 1911 the distribution was transferred to the Board of Education (ED 24/519 and UGC 7/1065) and handled by the Universities Branch established in 1910. The Board of Education had no administrative control over universities.

7.5   Asquith Commission

In 1907 the Bishop of Birmingham moved in the House of Lords the appointment of a royal commission to inquire how the endowments of Oxford and Cambridge could best be used to benefit all classes in the community. The commission did not begin work until after the First World War when all universities were experiencing financial difficulties with the influx of students and the post-war stringencies. The commissioners were asked to look into the financial resources of the colleges and halls. Papers relating to the work of the commissioners are in ED 24/528, 1190, 1940 and CAB 23/11, pp 110-112. They recommended the establishment of a statutory commission to carry out changes in statutes and to revise trusts. These recommendations were embodied in the Oxford and Cambridge Act 1923 which set up a commission for each university for two years. The papers of the Oxford commissioners survive in PC 10/21-49 and include minutes and correspondence with the Board of Education. PC 8/1279 contains petitions against the statutes. Bill papers are in ED 31/234-235, ED

24/988 and T 161/179/S16562, with Home Affairs Committee discussions in CAB 26/4-5 and the papers of the Privy Council committee on the Reconstruction of the Universities in PC 8/990. The application of the act to Keble College is considered in T 160/221/F8209.

7.6   University Grants Committee 1919-1989

The Board wished to rationalize the payment of these various grants to the universities and appointed a standing advisory committee to make recommendations for the allocation of the money. Reports, minutes and memoranda of the Advisory Committee on University Grants, 1911-1919 are in UGC 5/6-7. In November 1918 the President of the Board and the Chancellor of the Exchequer received a deputation from the universities about their financing (papers in UGC 5/8). In consequence, it was decided to increase government aid to university education and to amalgamate the various grants to universities and colleges. For this purpose the advisory committee was replaced in July 1919 by the University Grants Committee (UGC), a standing committee of the Treasury.

The UGC consisted of prominent men familiar with the work and needs of the universities. Its role was to advise the Treasury on the administration and allocation of grants to universities and university colleges. In practice this function extended to administrative responsibility for the allocation of university finance. The committee also provided information about university education and was involved in the preparation and execution of plans for the development of universities. In 1963 the UGC became responsible for grants to colleges of technology selected for expansion to university status in line with the recommendations of the Robbins Committee on Higher Education (ED 116; ED 117; ED 118 *and see chapter 5.7*).

Minutes of the committee are in UGC 1 and UGC 11, with agenda and papers to 1971 in UGC 2; the board's minutes, agenda and papers from 1972 are all in UGC 1. Annual reports of the committee, together with special reports on aspects of higher education, are in UGC 6 and UGC 3. Returns from institutions in receipt of grant are in UGC 3; schedules of the committee's expenditure on grants are in UGC 4. UGC 8 contains the minutes of various sub-committees, and UGC 9 their agenda and papers. Registered files of the committee are in UGC 7. Circular letters to university vice-chancellors are in UGC 7 and UGC 10.

7.7   Robbins Report

The Robbins Committee was appointed in 1960 by the Prime Minister, Harold Macmillan, to:

> review the pattern of full-time higher education in Great Britain and in the light of national needs and resources to advise Her Majesty's Government on what principles its long-term development should be based.

It reported in 1963 and its main recommendations included: that higher education in the UK should be expanded to meet the increasing demand of students qualified to enter; that opportunities for advanced work outside the universities should be extended to degree level in the arts, humanities and social studies as well as science and technology; that a new body be established to award degrees to students from courses at non-degree awarding institutions; and that new universities should be sited near large centres of population and should make generous provision for scientific and technology students. Information on the work of the committee is in ED 46/941-949; its agenda and minutes are in ED 116; evidence submitted to it and surveys conducted by it are in ED 118; and ED 117 contains other related papers.

Plans were already in place for an expansion of the university population: as early as 1956 the UGC had set a minimum target of 168,000 students by 1968; in 1957 it had set up its own sub-committee on new universities (UGC 7/169-172).

See also chapter 5.9.2.

7.8 Universities Branch

In December 1963 responsibility for the universities was transferred from the Treasury to the Lord President of the Council, but the universities management team remained part of the Treasury Social Services Division until the Office of the Minister for Science and the Ministry of Education were merged on 1 April 1964, to form the Department of Education and Science (DES). At that date a Universities Branch was formed within DES having two teams concerned respectively with finance and policy.

The financial team was directly responsible to the Treasury for the universities and colleges vote, although payments to the universities were made by DES Finance Branch on the advice of the UGC. The finance team also acquired the functions of the awards section of the former Ministry of Education, advising local authorities on grants for higher education, administering the issue of postgraduate awards in the humanities and, until 1969, handling the residual administration of the State Scholarship scheme. Postgraduate awards in science and technology were administered through the Research Councils.

Registered files on both financial and policy matters are available in ED 188. Policy matters covered include the new universities, colleges of advanced technology, the Open University, university research and the National Union of Students. They also contain information on two direct grant institutions, the Cranfield College of Technology and the Royal College of Art, as well as papers on the formation of the Computer Board for Universities and Research Councils.

7.9   List of Classes

Exchequer

1.   King's Remembrancer: Accounts Various Hen II-Geo III (E 101)
-    accounts of Warden of King's Hall, Cambridge, re expenses of scholars; some warrants and receipts for payment of annuities, etc by various Oxford and Cambridge colleges

2.   Court of Augmentations: Miscellaneous Books c1100-c1800 (E 315)
-    surveys of Oxford and Cambridge University 37 Henry VIII

Privy Council

1.   Unbound Papers 1481-1946 (PC 1)
-    charters to universities 19th and 20th centuries

2.   Original Correspondence 1860-1956 (PC 8)
-    university charters and statutes

3.   Records of Commissions, Committees and Court of Claims 1899-1937 (PC 10)
-    Statutory Commission for Oxford University 1923-1926; Departmental Committee on London University 1924-1925; Statutory Commission for London University 1926-1928

Treasury

1.   Treasury Board Papers 1557-1920 (T 1)
-    original correspondence on 19th century grants to universities

2.   Oxford University Commission 1854-1860 (T 73)
-    correspondence

3.   Treasury Deposit Accounts Ledgers 1918-1934 (T 252)
-    entries of income and expenditure including university college grants

Home Office

1.   Various Commissions: Records and Correspondence 1786-1918 (HO 73)
-    correspondence and draft reports of Oxford University Commission 1854-1858 and Cambridge University Commission 1856-1861

Education Departments

1.   Establishment Files 1835-1971 (ED 23)
        -       some working papers of Haldane Commission 1909-1913

2.   Private Office Papers 1851-1935 (ED 24)
        -       some working papers of Haldane Commission 1909-1913; H of C returns
                of parliamentary grant to universities; reports on grants of charters; bill
                papers

3   Universities and Colleges Endowment Files 1854-1944 (ED 39)
        -       mainly for scholarships and prizes and their administration under the
                Charitable Trusts Acts

4.   Bill Files 1869-1974 (ED 31)
        -       bill papers

5.   Expired Commissions: Durham University   1926-1937 (ED 112)
        -       papers of two inquiries

6.   Committee on Higher Education (Robbins Committee 1961-1963) Agenda and
        Minutes 1961-1963 (ED 116)
        -       bibliography and notes on composition of committee

7.   Committee on Higher Education (Robbins Committee 1961-1963) Papers 1961-
        1964 (ED 117)

8.   Committee on Higher Education (Robbins Committee 1961-1963): Surveys
        and Evidence 1961-1964 (ED 118)
        -       surveys by COI and private organizations of students at teacher training
                colleges, FE colleges, universities and children born 1940-1951;
                unpublished evidence; copy of report, appendixes and evidence

9.   Universities and University College Files 1874-1967 (ED 119)
        -       correspondence of university charters and statutes; distribution of
                government grants before UGC; proposals on ATOs after 1944

10.   Research and Planning General Files 1958-1975 (ED 181)
        -       establishment of National Council for Educational Technology

11.   Universities, Finance and Policy: Registered Files (H Series) 1952-1977 (ED
        188)
        -       new universities; colleges of advanced technology

University Grants Committee

1.   Minutes, Agenda and Papers 1919-1989 (UGC 1)

2.   Agenda and papers to 1971 1919-1971 (UGC 2)

3.   Returns 1919-1990 (UGC 3)
      -    grant returns from universities and university colleges; details of
           governing bodies, faculties, regulations, degrees, staff, students, finance
           and expenditure

4.   Departmental Expenditure Schedules 1921-1938 (UGC 4)
      -    schedules of grant expenditure by institution and purpose

5.   Miscellaneous Papers 1847-1942 (UGC 5)
      -    Board of Education reports, minutes and memoranda; papers of
           departmental committees; papers of Advisory Committee on University
           Grants 1911-1919; university deputation 23 Nov 1918; specimen file
           on provincial institutions 1936; university organization and finance in
           Second World War

6.   Reports and Annual Surveys 1919-1989 (UGC 6)
      -    irregular reports on UGC activities; annual reports from 1963; reports
           on specific topics

7.   Registered Files 1909-1988 (UGC 7)
      -    files covering all aspects of UGC work; circulars

8.   Subcommittee Minutes 1946-1989 (UGC 8)
      -    minutes of sub-committees dealing with fields of study, computers,
           superannuation, works and buildings, new university colleges

9.   Subcommittees, Agenda and Papers 1946-1977 (UGC 9)

10.   Circular Letters 1980-1989 (UGC 10)
      -    including statistics, procedural instructions and requests for information

11.   Signed Minutes 1919-1989 (UGC 11)

8.   SPECIAL SERVICES

8.1   Introduction

From the end of the nineteenth century there was a gradual development of services dealing with the health and physical condition of children. The Medical Branch of the Board of Education was set up in 1907. Its responsibilities included special educational treatment for handicapped children, the school medical service, the provision of school meals and (later) milk, the organization and inspection of physical training, maternity and infant welfare (transferred to the Ministry of Health in 1919) and nursery education. General files on all aspects of the work of the branch are in ED 50.

After the Second World War the branch was renamed the Special Services Branch and in 1974 its health functions were handed over to the National Health Service and its special educational functions were transferred to one of the Schools Branches.

8.2   Special Educational Treatment

From the middle of last century there is evidence in central government records that individual schools and school boards were taking an interest in education for handicapped children. In 1844, for example, the Yorkshire School for the Blind petitioned the Treasury for rent free accommodation for the school and suggested that the next census should include an assessment of the numbers of blind, deaf and dumb (T 1/4971/17853). The chairman of the London School Board attended a conference on the education of the deaf and dumb at Manchester School for the Deaf in 1891 and the board paid three guineas towards the cost of printing and distributing the conference papers (ED 14/25). ED 50/9 contains papers covering the period 1872 to 1893 urging the compulsory education of blind and deaf children as well as information about the arrangements made in London for the education of the blind and the appropriate training of their teachers.

The statutory foundation of special educational provision for handicapped children was laid in the last decade of the nineteenth century and evolved gradually until the Education Act 1944. The Elementary Education (Blind and Deaf Children) Act 1893 obliged every school authority to provide education for blind and deaf children between the ages of seven and sixteen resident in the area in some school certified for the purpose by the Education Department. The Elementary Education (Defective and Epileptic Children) Act 1899 empowered local authorities to provide for the training of physically and mentally defective and epileptic children. ED 14/43 gives details of the provision made by the London School Board in response to this legislation. Not all local authorities acted so promptly and so the Special Schools Education Act 1914 made the powers mandatory for mental defectives and epileptics. Further legislation in 1918 made provision obligatory for children with a physical handicap. Compulsory education for children suffering from these defects was extended to sixteen under the Education Act 1921.

Special educational provisions were re-enacted in sections 33 and 34 of the Education Act 1944 and modified in subsequent Acts of 1948 and 1953. Eleven, later ten, categories of handicap were identified: blind, partially sighted, deaf, partially deaf, delicate, diabetic, educationally sub normal, epileptic, maladjusted, physically handicapped, speech defects. New procedures were laid down in the Handicapped Pupils and School Health Service Regulations 1945 (ED 50/176) and later regulations. ED 152 contains local education authority schemes for post-war provision of special schools, eg Norfolk (ED 152/118). The equivalent files for Wales are in BD 7.

EXAMPLE:

BD 7/15, which covers the period 1947-1950, contains information on arrangements for special educational treatment in Merthyr Tydfil. The Ministry of Education comments that provision for handicapped pupils, ie blind, partially sighted, deaf, partially deaf, physically handicapped, epileptic and maladjusted children will have to be made on a national or a regional basis in agreement with the Welsh Joint Education Committee. Merthyr suggests co-operation with Brecon and Radnorshire to provide a boarding school for sixty delicate children. The Ministry also considers the need for a Day Open Air School for sufferers from anaemia, malnutrition, chronic bronchitis and those from homes with TB. Merthyr estimates that they have about one hundred children who are physically handicapped or Educationally Sub Normal (ESN); the Ministry indicates that one day school should be sufficient. Merthyr appoints its own speech therapist in March 1950.

The 1950s and 1960s saw the expansion of special educational provision catering for approximately two per cent of children. They tended to be housed in special schools, often former country houses remote from urban centres. There was very little contribution from mainstream to special education; this was not what Butler intended. The 1970 Education Act brought all handicapped children within special education and gave the LEAs a duty to educate them. This policy produced greater understanding and sensitivity in ordinary schools and the provision of more remedial teaching and more special units.

8.2.1 Warnock Report

A growing appreciation that handicap was more widespread than its narrow medical definition led to the announcement in 1973 by the Secretary of State for Education, Margaret Thatcher, of a national committee for special needs under Mary Warnock. The twenty-five members of the committee were appointed by the Labour administration in 1974 together with fifteen co-optees. The Committee of Inquiry into the Education of Handicapped Children and Young People met for more than three years and produced a 400 page report in 1978 with 224 recommendations.

The report stated that

> special education is about meeting individual needs and involves as much integration as possible and as much special help as necessary.

The report covered all aspects of special needs from pre-school to postgraduate research. It identified priority areas as under fives, sixteen plus and teacher training. The report was published as HC 1977-8 x Cmnd 7212 in May 1978. A far-reaching consultative exercise was begun which culminated in a white paper (*Special Needs in Education* HC 1980 Cmnd 7996) in 1980. This document promised no additional resources, was very cautious about commitments to the under fives, gave general encouragement to teacher training and said that further education would have to wait for 'a wider review of the legal framework'.

8.2.2   Special Educational Provision: the Education Act 1981

The 1981 Education Act was the legislative response to Warnock and was hailed as 'Warnock without resources'. Its main provisions were: the replacement of the category of handicapped pupil by special educational needs; the introduction of a statement of special needs for each such pupil; and an emphasis on integrated provision wherever possible. The three priority areas identified in Warnock (under fives, sixteen plus and teacher training) were not tackled in the legislation.

8.2.3   Records

Files on the formation of policy following legislation are in ED 50. ED 133 contains files dealing with the provision of special schools and related problems in particular education authorities. Files on individual special schools are in ED 32 for those in England and ED 224 for those in Wales. ED 38 contains the endowment files for special schools. Regulations for such schools and lists of certified schools for blind, deaf, handicapped and epileptic children were initially issued as Command Papers. ED 62 contains files relating to training establishments providing further education for handicapped persons, continuing instruction in special schools. Papers on boarding homes for maladjusted, educationally subnormal and diabetic children are in ED 122 (seventy-five year closure).

Early HMI reports on special schools are on the school files (ED 32 and ED 122). After 1948 they are in ED 195; the following abbreviations are used to distinguish the type of school:

DEL	Delicate
EP	Epileptic
ESN	Educationally sub-normal
MAL	Maladjusted
PD	Physically defective
PH	Physically handicapped
PS	Partially sighted

The class also includes more general reports and surveys relating to facilities available for special education in particular areas. ED 195/254, for example, contains a report written in 1962-1963 on a survey of deaf children transferred from special schools to mainstream schools.

8.3   School Health Service

The industrial revolution had increased the demand for a cheap supply of child labour; in the mines and factories children worked in appalling conditions and often suffered from poor health and inadequate nutrition. The introduction of compulsory education with the Education Act 1880 revealed a school population with malnutrition, ill health and physical defects. In 1890 the London School Board appointed a medical officer (ED 14/20 confirms such a post in 1895; ED 23/198 evidence in 1903 that LSB has had a MO for some years).

The Boer War 1899-1902 confirmed the poor physical condition of young recruits when between forty and sixty per cent of candidates failed their medicals. This led to the appointment of an interdepartmental committee on physical deterioration whose findings (HC 1904 xxii) were influential in the framing of the Education (Administrative Provisions) Act 1907 (bill papers ED 24/127-150; ED 31/151) and the Local Education Authorities (Medical Treatment) Act 1909 (bill papers ED 31/167; ED 29/95). This legislation led to the establishment of the school medical service.

Papers on the work of the Medical Branch and its relationship with the Inspectorate and other branches are in ED 50/4. HMIs were expected to be present at medical examinations of children when the Branch was first established (ED 24/228). Circulars on school medical inspection and the duties of school medical officers are available in ED 50/5-7. Some education authorities were innovative in their provision; from 1918 Westminster, for example, started experimental classes for stammerers (ED 14/105).

In 1919 the school medical service became the responsibility of the Ministry of Health. Under the Education Act 1944 it was renamed the school health service and free clinics were set up to provide treatment for minor ailments, speech therapy, chiropody, child guidance, orthopaedics, teeth, orthoptics and audiometry. Services for asthma, enuresis and rheumatism were also provided. Pupils were to be medically examined three times during their school life; failure to comply led to a £5 parental fine.

In 1932 a memorandum (no 552) was issued to inspectors on the health of school children. The returns, which formed the basis of a survey of the health of the school population, are in ED 109. The papers are arranged by local authority and described in the class list as '1932 reply to memorandum', eg ED 109/6733 (The Abbey School, Malvern Wells).

After the war the National Health Service (NHS) took over the school health service. From 1950 the responsibility was shared between the NHS and the education authorities. In 1973 the school health service was moved to the Area Health Authorities. There was a further reorganization in 1982/3 when it moved to the districts and regions.

General policy files on this service are in ED 50 codes 1 and 6 and ED 137 contains the related local education authority files.

8.4   School Meals Service

In 1889 the London School Board, concerned about the 'necessitous condition of the children due to want of proper nourishment' and the link with poor attendance, commissioned H R Appleton to investigate the scale of the problem (ED 14/24). Meals were provided for poor children by voluntary bodies. By 1905 the London County Council was running a 'dinner experiment' whereby food prepared at its cookery centres (*see chapter 11*) was used as cheap meals for school children (ED 14/93).

The Education (Provision of Meals) Act 1906 led to the development of the school meals service. Select committee papers on the bill are available in ED 24/106-109, other bill papers are in ED 24/105 and HLG 29/86, with related material in HLG 46/134-135. A copy of memorandum 57/1910 on school meals provision is in ED 22/10. The Education Act 1921 empowered LEAs to provide school meals for children who 'are unable by reason of lack of food to take full advantage of education provided for them'.

Until the outbreak of the Second World War, meals in elementary schools were provided almost exclusively for needy children. In 1939 it became national policy to provide a main mid-day meal in school for all children whose parents wanted them to have it. From 1940, LEAs were encouraged to extend and improve the meals service by the introduction of a government grant of seventy per cent and later ninety per cent of the cost. Advice on the nutritional content of meals was given in Board of Education circular 1571 of 12 November 1941 (ED 142/54).

The Education Act 1944 gave LEAs a statutory duty to provide school meals for all primary and secondary pupils who wanted them; the 1945 edition of the Provision of Milk and Meals Regulations set out the required standards for these meals. Subsidized milk had been introduced by the Milk in Schools Act 1934; it was freely provided from 1946. Full financial responsibility for the school meals service passed to the LEAs in 1967.

ED 50 contains general policy files on these services, with LEA files in ED 123. Information on the wartime service is in ED 138. Reports and surveys on the school meals service from 1954 to 1965 are in ED 194; subjects covered include the nutritional value of the meals, the kitchens and utensils and the supervision of the kitchen staff and the children.

8.5   Physical Training

Military drill appeared in the Code of 1871 and physical instruction along Scandinavian lines was introduced into elementary schools towards the end of the nineteenth century. The first training college for female physical education instructors was opened in Dartford in 1885 (*see chapter 9*).

Under both the 1918 and 1921 Acts, local authorities were permitted to promote both social and physical training, supplementing that provided for children attending public elementary schools and for those under eighteen attending educational institutions. Facilities provided included evening swimming lessons, theatre visits and music festivals, school camps and school journeys. Local education authority files on this provision are in ED 101, with papers relating to the appropriate section of the Education Acts in the Elementary Education, General Files in ED 11.

The Physical Training and Recreation Act 1937 extended this provision to young persons and adults not in full-time attendance at schools or educational institutions. The extension was suspended for the duration of the war and the 1944 Act again limited the use of the facilities to those attending educational institutions. Papers on the provision by LEAs of community centres, playing fields, swimming baths, recreation centres and courses during the short-lived period of extension, 1937-1940, are in ED 56. Responsibility for post-school social and recreational training passed to the Further Education Branch of the Ministry of Education on its creation in 1945.

8.6   Nursery Education

Nursery schools were first established by voluntary effort at the beginning of this century. The Education Acts 1918 and 1921 permitted LEAs to supply or aid the supply of nursery schools and classes for children between two and five years of age; conditional grant-aid was made available in 1919. Files on individual nursery schools and their recognition for grant purposes are in ED 69.

The development of nursery provision was hampered by the Depression. The need for expansion was encouraged by a joint Ministry of Health and Board of Education circular of 1929, urged by the report of the Consultative Committee on Infant and Nursery Education in 1933, under the chairmanship of Sir W H Hadow (committee papers ED 10/149-150) and further emphasized by an LEA survey of 1936 on the requirement for nursery provision for the under-fives.

The Second World War led to the establishment of nursery centres in reception areas, day nurseries for the children of women war workers (ED 66/59-145) and the provision of evening play centres for children of school age (ED 65). Section 8(2) of the 1944 Act sought to extend the provision of nursery schools and classes, where appropriate, and LEAs were asked to include such provision in their development plans (ED 152). The clause remained practically inoperative.

LEA files on nursery education, including papers on the 1936 survey, are in ED 66; many of the papers between 1945 and 1955 are joint reports on nurseries by HM Inspectors and Public Health Nursing Officers; for the period 1956-1966 sample files from five local education authorities have been preserved (Gloucestershire, Nottinghamshire, London, Barnsley and Bootle). Departmental policy files are in ED 102.

8.7   List of Classes

8.7.1   Institution Files

1.   Special Services: Special School Files 1894-1973 (ED 32)
     - applications for recognition and grant; inspection reports

2.   Elementary Education: Nursery School Files   1918-1969 (ED 69)
     - recognition for grant, visits by departmental representatives, accounts

3.   Welsh Department: Special Schools Files (M and WM Series) 1904-1976 (ED 224)

4.   Special Services: Training Establishments for Handicapped Persons 1902-1956 (ED 62)
     - organization, curricula; fees; recognition for grants; inspectors' reports

5.   Special Services: Evening Play Centre Files 1917-1938 (ED 65)
     - provision for recreation after school hours; recognition for grants; inspectors' reports; annual reports of voluntary bodies

6.   Special Services: Boarding Homes for Children: Files1932-1970 (ED 122) (closed for 75 years)
     - inspectors' reports; recognition of homes

8.7.2   Endowment Files

1.   Special Services Endowment Files 1859-1944 (ED 38)
    -    administration of endowments; schemes and orders

8.7.3   Local Education Authority Files

1.   Social and Physical Training, Local Education Authority Files 1919-1944 (ED 101)
    -    approval for school trips, camps, acquisition and equipping of buildings and playing fields

2.   Special Services: Local Education Authorities, Special Education Treatment Files 1900-1956 (ED 133)
    -    provision of special schools for physically and mentally handicapped, blind, deaf and epileptic children

3.   Special Services: School Health Services Local Education Authority Files 1924-1972 (ED 137)
    -    reports by inspectors and medical officers of the department; annual reports of school medical officers and school dental service; staffing returns; wartime and special services

4.   Special Services: Local Education Authority: School Meals Service Files 1918-1969 (ED 123)
    -    reports of special services; reports of school medical officers; free or cheap milk schemes

5.   Nursery Education: Local Education Authority Files 1918-1966 (ED 66)
    -    proposals for nursery schools and classes; reports on areas; 1936 survey

8.7.4   General Files

1.   Special Services, General Files 1872-1974 (ED 50)
    -    provision and administration of special educational facilities for physically and mentally handicapped children; school meals service; school health service

2.   Nursery Education, General Files   1917-1968 (ED 102)
    -    draft regulations, circulars and memoranda, legal decisions, policy correspondence with other departments

9. TEACHERS

9.1 Training schools

Teacher training, like other educational initiatives, started in the voluntary sector. In the early nineteenth century, Joseph Lancaster began training students to teach in his private school at Borough Road, Southwark and built a hostel alongside. This was the prototype British Society training school. In 1812 the National Society followed suit and opened a school for training masters in Baldwin Gardens, off Gray's Inn Road (later moved to Westminster). Both used a form of the monitorial system of teaching.

Between them the two Societies had a significant and lasting effect on the recruitment, training and service of teachers in public elementary schools until the end of the century. The ignorant state of applicants caused the National Society to insist not only on a certificate of basic qualifications or an entry examination but also on a final examination and a probationary teaching period before the award of a Teacher's Certificate. The British Society decided that the main components of the curriculum should be English grammar, good handwriting, arithmetic, geography and history, with other subjects when time permitted.

9.2 Training College building grants

In 1834 Lord Brougham secured the appointment of a select committee to inquire into popular education (HC 1834 ix). He told the committee that it was the government's duty to train teachers in elementary schools and suggested that four normal (training) schools be established in London, Exeter, Lancaster and York. In 1835 the Home Secretary, Lord John Russell, persuaded Parliament to grant £10,000 in aid of building normal schools; the money was used by the British and National Societies. Building grants for training colleges were authorized by Privy Council Minutes of 1843 and 1844 (ED 17/1). Further information will be found in T 1 and ED 103/140 and ED 40 (*see chapter 12 for details*).

As secretary to the PC Committee on Education, Dr James Kay-Shuttleworth encouraged voluntary bodies to secure grants for training college construction. Simultaneously, from private resources and with help from E Carleton Tufnell and local clergy, he set up a training school for schoolmasters at Battersea; the original aim being to provide well-trained teachers for pauper schools. In 1841 he applied to the Treasury for help towards the expenses of establishing Battersea Normal School. The PCCE supported Kay's application, claiming that 'its work will benefit the Poor Law Commission and other public institutions' (T 1/4595/13542). Battersea was successful in adapting continental reforms to English conditions, preparing textbooks and testing and modifying methods of training teachers. It remained a private venture for four years until taken over by the National Society.

In 1847 the PCCE bought an estate called Kneller Hall at Whitton in Middlesex for £10,500 to convert to a Normal School for the education of schoolmasters. The work took four years to complete. (C 54/13618, nos 4-5; T 1/5313/27240, 5422/26206, 5689A/22429 *and see chapter 12*). A register of letters received and dispatched relating to Kneller Hall for the years 1852-1853 survives (ED 9/23).

By the late 1840s, thirty training colleges had been established; twenty-five were Church of England; all were residential; most had fewer than seventy-five students. Five claimed to provide three year courses but most offered only one year. Information about these colleges maintained by voluntary bodies is in ED 78, but few papers prior to 1932 have survived. The calibre of student was often poor both physically and intellectually. The limitations of the old monitorial system were well understood and the connection had been established between educational efficiency and competent teachers.

9.3   Pupil-Teachers

Kay-Shuttleworth was largely responsible for introducing a new system of pupil-teachers into this country. He had been an assistant poor law commissioner in East Anglia. At Gressenhall, one of the workhouses for which he was responsible, Dr Kay saw a thirteen-year-old boy taking over the class when the schoolmaster was sick. It is said that this gave him the idea for the pupil-teacher system. However, Kay had travelled extensively both in Scotland and on the continent, observing different teaching methods, including the statutory system of pupil-teachers practised in Holland since 1816. While Kay was an assistant commissioner working in East Anglia in 1838 he sent a report to the Poor Law Commissioners on *The Training of Pauper Children* in which he recommends the adoption of a pupil-teacher scheme he has observed in Haarlem (MH 32/49, paper 11109a).

Dr Kay was able to test out his ideas at the large workhouse at Norwood in south London, which contained over a thousand children. With the co-operation of the proprietor and a grant of £500 from the Home Office, Kay reorganized the school, grouping the pupils into classes of forty, erecting partitions for classrooms, building workshops, acquiring a naval instructor and appointing pupil-teachers. This experiment was so successful that in 1846 the PCCE launched a pupil-teacher scheme devised by Kay (ED 17/9).

Pupil-teachers were apprenticed to the headmaster for five years (thirteen to eighteen) and examined annually by HMIs on a prescribed, graded syllabus. Participants were paid. At eighteen the students sat for a competitive exam and successful candidates

LIVERPOOL JOHN MOORES UNIVERSITY
LEARNING SERVICES

were awarded a Queen's Scholarship entitling them to a three year course at training college. After college they qualified as certificated teachers.

Kay saw the scheme as a first step but many did not attempt to go on to normal school. The teacher's certificate was made available to serving teachers by examination, without a normal school training. Public elementary schools became staffed to a large extent by ex-pupil-teachers.

The pupil-teacher system received a setback with the issuing of the Revised Code in 1862. The block grant system replaced specific grants, the syllabus was reduced, Queen's Scholarships were abolished, the quality and numbers of applicants fell, two training colleges closed. However, in the five years following the Elementary Education Act 1870 the school population doubled and more teachers for public elementary schools were urgently required. The voluntary societies responded by opening more training colleges and the PCCE restored grants for exam results and Queen's Scholarships, allowed colleges to pass students out after one year and permitted HMIs to award teaching certificates without examination. In the decade between 1870 and 1880 pupil-teachers doubled, the number of certificated teachers trebled and assistant teachers (those without a certificate, often ex-pupil-teachers) multiplied seven times.

The London General Files (ED 14/18-19,24-26,31) provide useful information on the working of the pupil-teacher system in the metropolis from 1870 to the turn of the century. Covering a similar period, ED 11/31 includes departmental correspondence about pupil-teachers with the Roman Catholic Poor Schools Committee. Several memoranda on the history, working and prospects of the pupil-teacher system at the beginning of the twentieth century survive among the Private Office Papers (ED 24/68A,429,434,436) including one written by Robert Morant, secretary to the Board of Education from 1902 (ED 24/76).

9.4   Pupil-Teacher Centres

There was concern about the standard of teaching in elementary schools with these numbers of uncertificated staff and the influx of pupils. In consequence, school boards like London and Liverpool in urban areas, began to develop their own pupil-teacher centres where teachers collected for instruction, at first in the evenings and on Saturdays. The general files of the London School Board (ED 14) illustrate these developments.

EXAMPLE:

ED 14/31 contains the details of a scheme established in Greenwich in 1875 for the collective instruction of pupil-teachers in the area. Two centres were to be set up, one

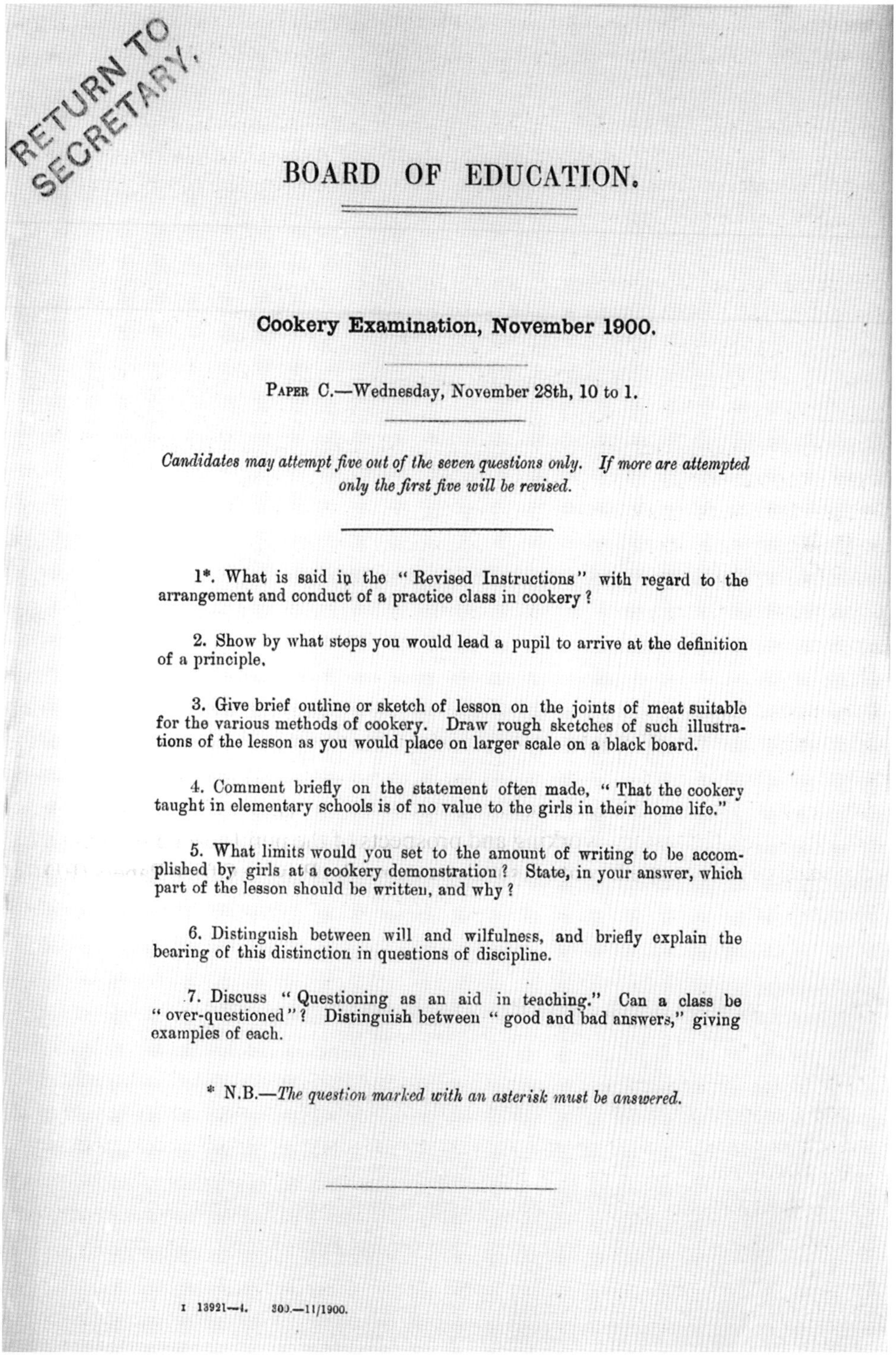

RETURN TO SECRETARY.

BOARD OF EDUCATION.

Cookery Examination, November 1900.

PAPER C.—Wednesday, November 28th, 10 to 1.

Candidates may attempt five out of the seven questions only. If more are attempted only the first five will be revised.

1*. What is said in the " Revised Instructions" with regard to the arrangement and conduct of a practice class in cookery ?

2. Show by what steps you would lead a pupil to arrive at the definition of a principle.

3. Give brief outline or sketch of lesson on the joints of meat suitable for the various methods of cookery. Draw rough sketches of such illustrations of the lesson as you would place on larger scale on a black board.

4. Comment briefly on the statement often made, " That the cookery taught in elementary schools is of no value to the girls in their home life."

5. What limits would you set to the amount of writing to be accomplished by girls at a cookery demonstration ? State, in your answer, which part of the lesson should be written, and why ?

6. Distinguish between will and wilfulness, and briefly explain the bearing of this distinction in questions of discipline.

7. Discuss " Questioning as an aid in teaching." Can a class be " over-questioned"? Distinguish between " good and bad answers," giving examples of each.

* N.B.—*The question marked with an asterisk must be answered.*

ɪ 13921—4. 300.—11/1900.

Figure 12
Example of a departmental cookery exam for pupil-teachers, November 1900 (ED 24/68A)

for females and one for males. The pupil-teachers were to meet on Mondays, Wednesdays and Fridays from 6-8pm. Subject syllabuses for the centre are included on the file.

The London School Board raised the age of male pupil-teachers to fifteen in 1875 and of females in 1881. Three years later it abolished compulsory instruction for pupil-teachers outside school hours and reduced their teaching time to three hours per day. The pupil-teacher centres became specialized types of school. ED 11/2 contains papers on the provision and legal status of pupil-teacher centres for the period 1901-1908 and ED 24/68A includes a breakdown of the numbers of pupil-teachers attending the centres at the turn of the century. Board of Education List 62 gives details of all pupil-teacher centres, eg ED 12/308 for 1913.

Surviving pupil-teacher centre files are in ED 57. They represent only centres which were conducted independently of any particular school. The papers on these files include proposals to establish centres, acquisition of sites and premises, alterations and enlargements to existing centres, requests for loans and sales of buildings. Information about arrangements for Welsh pupil-teachers and the establishment of pupil-teacher centres from 1900 is in ED 93.

The Cross Commission 1886-1888 looked at the whole question of pupil-teachers and teacher training (*see 3.5*). It produced minority and majority reports: the former called for fundamental changes in the pupil-teacher system, the latter upheld existing arrangements with minor improvements. In 1896, the PCCE set up a departmental committee under the Rev T W Sharpe, senior chief inspector, 'to inquire into the workings of the Pupil-Teacher system'. Its report, two years later, recommended reform (HC 1898 xxvi). The committee recognized the need of all pupil-teachers to receive secondary education and suggested that the best pupil-teacher centres should convert to secondary schools.

9.5   University training departments

The files of the London School Board contain evidence that board school pupil-teachers, who were Queen's scholars, could not obtain a place in a residential training college because there were too few places and too many denominational restrictions (ED 14/19). The Cross Commission accepted that this experience was duplicated across the country and recommended an experiment in non-residential training colleges to be set up by universities, not school boards (ED 10/42).

In 1890 the Education Department authorized universities and university colleges to set up training departments where student teachers could read for degrees. Departments opened at King's College, London, Owen's College, Manchester, Oxford and Cambridge. By 1901 seventeen departments of this type were established and from

1911 a four year course was introduced: three years for a degree and the fourth for teacher training. Files on university teacher training departments are in ED 81, but no material survives before 1932. The university and university college files (ED 119) include information on the distribution of grants for special purposes, such as teacher training, prior to the establishment of the University Grants Committee in 1919 (*see 7.6*).

9.6 Secondary School Teachers

The development of training for secondary school teachers during the nineteenth century was largely at the instigation of women. Frances Mary Buss, mother of the headmistress of North London Collegiate, persuaded the Home and Colonial College to introduce training for secondary teachers in 1845. The College of Preceptors, founded in 1846, had facilities for the professional training of secondary school teachers; it started training courses in 1873 and established a training department for secondary teachers in 1895. ED 24/1816 contains a memorandum about the college. Miss Buss became the first woman on the council of the College of Preceptors and persuaded the college to start classes for secondary teachers under Joseph Payne, the first Professor of Education. Dorothea Beale, at Cheltenham, supported a training college for women to teach in secondary schools and forged the link with Oxford where the college expanded into St Hilda's and became a hall of the university. Maria Grey, founder of the Girls Public Day School Trust, started a training college for women secondary school teachers at Brondesbury, which was later moved to Twickenham. The GPDST aimed to provide facilities for student teachers under its headmistresses.

The Schools Inquiry (Taunton) Commission (*see 4.2.2*) decided against training for secondary school teachers. Sir James Kay-Shuttleworth assembled a committee representing the public schools, training colleges and HMIs to declare in favour. The Headmasters' Conference, after years of regular debate, persuaded Cambridge to start a teacher training syndicate in 1879; women used it, men did not.

The involvement of universities in day training for elementary school teachers after 1890 and the cautious endorsement of the Bryce Commission (*see 4.2.4* and ED 12/ 11-12) encouraged the development of secondary training in the university departments. Real impetus was given to the movement by the Education Act 1902, which enabled the establishment of county or municipal secondary schools. The new schools, often evolving from pupil-teacher centres, created a demand for well-qualified graduate teachers.

9.7 Education Act 1902

The recent legislation enabled Robert Morant, secretary to the Board of Education, to issue the first regulations for the Instruction and Training of Pupil-Teachers and

Students in Training Colleges in 1903. Information about the framing of these and later regulations for teachers is in ED 86. The minimum age for pupil-teachers was raised to sixteen (except in some rural areas), their hours of teaching were restricted, participation in approved courses of instruction in recognized pupil-teacher centres was made obligatory and wherever possible secondary education was encouraged. Pupil-teacher centres were to be improved and more closely monitored. The King's Scholarship was replaced by the Preliminary Examination for Elementary School Teachers Certificate. Bursaries were introduced in 1907 for selected pupils to remain a further year at school between sixteen and eighteen and then to enter training college (ED 24/430,433). These measures marked the end of the pupil-teacher system, which was virtually extinct by the First World War.

The 1902 Act enabled LEAs to provide and maintain training colleges. This was to help the continuing unmet demand for training college places. LEAs were slow to take up this option, although the introduction of seventy-five per cent capital grants for buildings provided some encouragement; there were still no maintenance grants. By 1914 twenty non-denominational municipal colleges had opened (out of 146 local authorities). Information about these building grants is in ED 87 (*see also chapter 12*); general policy files on grant-aid for training colleges are in ED 86. Files on training colleges established by LEAs under the provisions of the 1902 act are in ED 78; few papers survive before 1932. ED 67 contains files on the arrangements made by LEAs for the training and supply of teachers; little material survives before 1924, except for some staff returns of teachers in Welsh elementary schools. Other LEA schemes for teacher training under the 1902 Act are in ED 53. Files concerning the LEA provision of short courses for teachers at further education colleges, art schools and evening institutes are in ED 61; material prior to 1935 has not survived. The registered files in ED 192 continue the teachers' general files in ED 86 and ED 108. There are separate series of Welsh Department files for teacher training colleges in Wales (ED 217) and for staffing Welsh schools (ED 218).

9.8   Burnham Committee

In 1923 Edward Wood, President of the Board of Education, set up a departmental committee on the Training of Teachers for Elementary Schools, under Lord Burnham, (HC 1924-5 xii; ED 24/1193, 1201, 1814, 1818). In its sixty-nine recommendations it called for greater co-operation between training colleges and universities. One tangible result was the establishment of Joint Examination Boards (JEBs), described in Board of Education circular 1372 of 11 January 1925 (ED 142/50). These consisted of representatives from universities, training colleges, LEAs and HMIs to devise and conduct the final examination in academic subjects on which the teaching certificate was awarded. The Board of Education continued to be responsible for testing teaching practice. The JEB files are in ED 105.

In August 1930, under circular 1480 (ED 142/51), a Central Advisory Committee for the Certification of Teachers was appointed. All interested bodies were represented and its function was to hold a watching brief over the examinations conducted by the JEBs and to advise the Board of Education.

9.9 Teachers in rural areas

The first regulations for teacher training (*see 9.1 above*) acknowledged that there were particular problems in rural areas. The acceptance of the Burnham Committee recommendation that intending teachers should remain in full time secondary education until eighteen was known to be impractical in country districts. In 1927, therefore, another departmental committee was set up to examine the training of rural teachers. Its investigations showed that outside the towns it was usual for only half the practising teachers to be certificated (ED 24/1815; ED 86/47).

The committee recommended that a core of academic subjects should be common to the studies of all intending teachers but that there should also be special courses for those wishing to teach in country schools. The effect of its report was diminished by the Depression. Files in ED 67, however, reflect the difficulties of teacher training in rural districts:

ED 67/3	1939-1941	Berkshire
ED 67/9	1946-1947	Derbyshire
ED 67/31	1937-1938	Norfolk
ED 67/35	1928-1949	Nottinghamshire
ED 67/43	1939-1945	East Suffolk
ED 67/50	1937-1939	Westmorland
ED 6753	1926-1932	Worcestershire
ED 67/56	1928-1931	Yorkshire (NR)

9.10 McNair Committee

R A Butler, President of the Board of Education, wishing to expand post-war education and to raise the school leaving age, appointed a committee in 1942 to investigate the supply, training and recruitment of teachers (ED 86/94-109). It reported two years later and advised that an additional 70,000 teachers would be required. It recommended that the conditions of service and salaries of teachers should be improved (*see 9.13 below*) and that the two year courses at training colleges should be extended to three.

The committee also saw the need for a closer relationship between universities and training colleges and put forward two schemes for co-ordinated training: either developing the university schools of education; or extending the JEB system (ED 136/608, 714). The majority of Area Training Organizations (ATOs), as they were known, finally adopted the first version and set up Institutes of Education (Birmingham, Bristol, Durham, Exeter, Nottingham, Hull, Leicester, London, Manchester, Southampton, Wales, Sheffield, Leeds and Oxford); others adapted a version of the second scheme, known as scheme C (Cambridge, Reading and Liverpool). Some papers on the formation ATOs are in ED 119, listed by university; other material is in ED 159, arranged in alphabetical order of participating institute.

9.11   Emergency Training Scheme

The debate over post-war education in the early 1940s (*see 4.6*), the wish to reduce class sizes, the anticipation of an increase in pupils and the loss of teachers during the war all contributed to the appointment in 1943, by R A Butler, President of the Board of Education, of an advisory committee to consider how to meet the post-war need for teachers. The committee, under the chairmanship of G N (later Sir Gilbert) Fleming, assistant secretary to the Board, included departmental civil servants and representatives from the LEAs and teachers' associations. The provisional scheme for the emergency recruitment and training of teachers, which the committee produced, is outlined in circular 1652 of 15 May 1944 (ED 142/54). Papers relating to the work of the committee are in ED 143/1-5, with related material in ED 136/687-688.

The scheme was piloted at Goldsmiths' College in September 1944 (ED 143/32) and the first emergency training college opened the following year. By December 1947, fifty-five such colleges were running. It began to be run down in 1949 and the last course ended in 1951. The scheme is described in Ministry of Education pamphlet No 17, *Challenge and Response* (HMSO, 1950). A copy is available in ED 143/37. It produced 35,000 qualified teachers and made practical raising the school leaving age to fifteen in 1947.

The papers in ED 143 contain policy decisions leading to the scheme and its administration. They also include information on special courses for uncertificated teachers. Representative emergency college files have been preserved for Alnwick in Northumberland (ED 143/33-34) and Borthwick Training College for Women in London (ED 143/35-36).

9.12   Post-war developments

Teacher training colleges were expanded after the Second World War, quite apart from the emergency training scheme. Fifty per cent and later one hundred per cent grants were offered to LEAs for the expansion and refurbishment of existing colleges and the establishment of new ones. In 1939 there were sixty-three voluntary and twenty-eight LEA colleges, by 1951 fifty-six voluntary and seventy-six LEA colleges were open. After 1968 financial matters pertaining to teacher training were administered by pooling committees run by the Department of Education and Science Finance Branch; their minutes and papers can be found in ED 198.

Ministry of Education Pamphlet No 34 *The Training of Teachers* (HMSO, 1957) suggested a three year training college course. The Minister referred the matter to the National Advisory Council (*see 9.15 below*) and September 1960 was chosen as the date for introduction. ED 86/454 contains the papers of the sub-committee on the scope and content of the three year course. The Willis-Jackson Committee looked at the supply and training of teachers for technical colleges between 1957 and 1959 (ED 46/972-977).

The Crowther Report 1959 (*see 4.8 above*) recommended that efforts should be made to attract graduates to the teaching profession. This view was echoed by Robbins Report (*see 5.9.2 and 7.7 above*) which called for closer links with the universities, and for teacher training colleges to be renamed Colleges of Education with four year courses leading to a B.Ed degree (*see chapter 11*). In 1966 a study group was appointed, under T R (later Sir Toby) Weaver, to investigate the government of Colleges of Education (ED 86/359-361). It recommended independent governing bodies and the formation of academic boards with delegated powers. Circular 18 of 1969 (ED 142/23) required that in future graduates teaching in the maintained sector must be trained (for primary teachers from December 1969 and secondary teachers from December 1973).

In 1970 a committee of inquiry, under the chairmanship of Lord James of Rusholme, was appointed by the Education Secretary, Margaret Thatcher, to look at ATOs (*see 9.10 above*) and teacher training. The James Committee made six main recommendations: the expansion of in-service training; planned reinforcement of the induction process; an all graduate profession; the improvement of teacher-training in further education; the complete acceptance of colleges of education into higher education; and improved arrangements for the control and co-ordination of teacher-training and supply, both nationally and regionally. The minutes, papers and correspondence of the James Committee are in ED 145.

The white paper *Education: A Framework for Expansion* of December 1972 accepted these recommendations (HC 1972-3 vii, 1013 Cmnd 5174), but circular 7/73 *Development of Higher Education in the non-University Sector* (ED 142/27) made it clear that the future of most colleges of education was on the non-university sector side of the binary line in higher education. In effect, by about 1975 the McNair arrangements for teacher training were ending; the ATOs were declining; teacher education and certain institutions of advanced further education were amalgamating.

9.13   Teachers' Pay and Conditions

The interest of central government in teachers has largely been confined to the issue of supply, although it has necessarily been concerned with qualification, payment, pensions and conduct. Before 1921 there were no standard pay scales for teachers;

each school or LEA made its own arrangements. Conditions improved to some degree after the Education Act 1902 and again in 1917 when H A L Fisher, President of the Board, secured an increase in the Exchequer contribution to teachers' salaries.

The recommendations of a departmental committee on the construction of salary scales in 1918 (HC 1917-18 xi Cmnd 8939; ED 24/1779,1780; ED 11/33-34) enabled Fisher, the following year, to set up a committee under Lord Burnham, on which teachers and LEAs were also represented, to work out nationally based scales for elementary school teachers. Other similar committees were formed to consider the pay of secondary and technical teachers. These bodies became known as the Burnham Committees and, after Lord Burnham's death in 1933, the title was officially adopted.

The committees were reconstituted and the scales recast to meet the requirements of the Education Act 1944 and of the McNair Committee (*see 9.10 above*); the distinction between elementary and secondary teachers was abolished; extra allowances were introduced for special qualifications or duties. In 1963 the Minister of Education insisted that additional monies available went to heads of grammar schools. This caused a revision of the Burnham Committees, adding ministerial representation.

ED 108 contains minutes of Burnham committee meetings, policy papers relating to teachers' salaries and educational economy measures (ED 108/59-63). Other related papers are in ED 86 and ED 24. Files on teachers' superannuation are in ED 131 and ED 24 code 52/7, with related material in ED 10/86B and ED 14/91. Post-1961 papers on pay and conditions will be found in ED 192.

The suspension or cancellation of a teacher's certificate renders the individual unable to teach. This power was available to the Education Department over elementary school teachers in grant-aided schools under the Education Act 1870. The Elementary School Teachers' (Superannuation) Act 1898 made the restoration of the certificate a condition of continued receipt of benefits. Under another Superannuation Act 1918 misconduct resulted in loss of benefits. Withdrawal of recognition from technical school teachers became possible under the Technical Regulations in 1910 and the Education Act 1921 imposed similar conditions on secondary school teachers. The co-operation of independent schools in excluding unsuitable persons from teaching was secured in 1957 (ED 104/14).

Papers on the procedure for cancelling or suspending teachers' certificates and policy files on the treatment of cases of teachers' misconduct are in ED 104 (some pieces closed for fifty or seventy-five years). ED 12/529 includes correspondence for the period 1936-1943 on the right of teachers to be heard before dismissal. ED 24 code 52/4 lists other papers dating from 1909 to 1930 on teachers' misconduct, eg ED 24/1771 covering office procedure.

For use of the Committee only.

BOARD OF EDUCATION.

Provisional Minimum Scales as laid down by the
Standing Joint Committee.

Certificated Head Teachers.

Men.		Women.
Grade I (1-100) A.T.+ £20-£12½-£330		A.T. + £15 - £12½ - £264.
" II(101-200)A.T.+ £40-£12½-£366		A.T. + £30 - £12½ - £288.
" III(201-350)A.T.+£60-£12½-£390.		A.T. + £45 - £12½ - £312.
" IV(351-500)A.T.+£80-£12½-£420.		A.T. + £60 - £12½ - £336.
" V(501 & over) A.T.+£100-£12½-£450.		A.T. + £75 - £12½ - £360.
Schools a.a.40 or under A.T.+ £10-£12½ -£315.		A.T. + £10 - £12½ - £253½

Certificated Assistant Teachers.

Collegiate -	£160 - £10 - £300		£150 - £10 - £240.
Non Collegiate -	£150 - £10 - £300.		£140 - £10 - £240.

Uncertificated Head Teachers.

Minimum.	Uncertd.Asst. + £10.	Uncertd.Asst. + £10.
Maximum.	Uncertd.Asst. + £15.	Uncertd.Asst. + £12.
Increments.	£6.	£6.

Uncertificated Assistant Teachers.

Apptd. prior to 1st April 1914. Maximum £180-£6.		Maximum £150 - £6.
" subsequent " " £100-£6-£150.		£90-£6-£140.

Teachers of Special Subjects.

Certd. or

Handicraft (Fully qualified Teachers)   Domestic Science (Fully
                                                              qualified teachers)

Same scale as for Non Collegiate   Same scale as for Women
Assistant Teachers.   Collegiate Assistant Teachers.

Figure 13
First proposed Burnham pay scale, 1919 (ED 108/11)

ROYAL SOCIETY OF TEACHERS

EXECUTIVE: THE TEACHERS REGISTRATION COUNCIL AS ESTABLISHED BY ACT OF PARLIAMENT 1907
AND CONSTITUTED BY ORDERS IN COUNCIL FEBRUARY 1912 AND DECEMBER 1926

This is to Certify that

Maud Gertrude Elliott,

having complied with the Conditions of Registration prescribed by the Council under the above mentioned Orders has been duly Registered as a Teacher and admitted as a Member of the Royal Society of Teachers

Register Number

11354

Date October 1915

Authorised by
The Teachers Registration Council
On behalf of the
Royal Society of Teachers

Frank Roscoe Secretary

Figure 14
Royal Society of Teachers certificate awarded to Miss Maud Gertrude Elliott, 1915
Below: Miss Maud Elliott (Both items courtesy of Roger Nixon)

9.14   Teachers' Registration Council

The Board of Education Act 1899 made provision for the establishment of a register of teachers, following one of the recommendations of the Bryce Commission (*see 4.2.4*). The Teachers' Registration Council was set up in 1902. The form in which the register was kept led to protests by the National Union of Teachers, resulting in its withdrawal in 1907; the Council was not reconstituted until 1912. The Council was independent of the Board of Education; it issued lists of teachers in alphabetical order; registration was voluntary. Neither the Board nor the LEAs used it in selecting candidates for promotion and, consequently, its success remained limited. The Teachers' Registration Council was succeeded by the Royal Society of Teachers (which was granted its Royal Charter in 1929) although the members of the Council remained as the Society's executive committee. Registration was abandoned in 1948 and the Council was dissolved the following year. Its minute books, together with copies of its reports for the years 1902 to 1906, are in ED 44; further papers relating to its work are among the General Education, General Files (ED 10/48-53,57-67,69-70,132-133,205).

9.15   National Advisory Council on the Training and Supply of Teachers

Following the recommendations of the McNair Report (*see above 9.10*), the Minister set up an interim committee to ensure that the supply of, and demand for, teachers matched. Its members were drawn from the schools, training colleges, university education departments and LEAs. By 1949 the interim committee became the National Advisory Council on the Training and Supply of Teachers (NACTST) and worked through two standing committees: one for training and qualifications; the second for recruitment and distribution. It produced eleven reports concerned with both general questions of training and supply and with more specialized problems, eg training to teach handicapped children. Papers on its activities will be found in ED 86/207-285 and 448-459. Registered files on the NACTST are in ED 192 and include material on the shortage of mathematics and science teachers and encouraging married women to return to teaching.

9.16   List of Classes

9.16.1   Institution Files

1.   Building Grant Applications 1833-1881 (ED 103)
    -        including applications for grants towards cost of erection of training colleges and practising schools; estimates of income and expenditure; details of tenure

2. School Board Office and Pupil Teacher Centre Files 1884-1911 (ED 57)
   - proposals and schemes; acquisition, development and sale of sites and premises; loan applications

3. Teacher Training College Files 1924-1975 (ED 78)
   - provision, maintenance and administration of training colleges and university colleges with teacher training courses

4. Teachers University Training Departments: Files 1932-1961 (ED 81)
   - liaison between Board of Education and Universities; organization of University Departments and their co-operation with other colleges; courses

5. Universities and University College Files 1874-1967 (ED 119)
   - including files on teacher training courses; area training organization (from 1944)

6. Welsh Department: Teacher Training Institutions Files (WR Series) 1929 - 1969 (ED 217)
   - student ratios, use of Welsh, expansion, buildings, finance

7. Teacher Training Colleges: Endowment Files 1858-1945 (ED 40)
   - administration of endowments; schemes and orders

8. Teacher Training Colleges: Building Grant Files 1904-1924 (ED 87)
   - acquisition, erection and improvement of premises

9. Teachers: Area Training Organization Files 1947-1963 (ED 159)
   - staff; premises; annual reports; schemes of government; courses of study; board of governors' papers; academic boards' papers

10. Emergency Recruitment and Training of Teachers 1943-1952 (ED 143)
    - includes representative files on two colleges

9.16.2   Local Authority Files

1. Teachers' Short Courses, Local Education Authority Files 1934-1954 (ED 61)
   - provision of courses at further education colleges, art schools, evening institutes, etc; inspectors' reports

2.   Teachers: Local Education Authority Supply Files 1912-1949 (ED 67)
  -    local facilities; reports on training; pupil teacher centres; pupil teachers in rural areas; statistics

3.   Finance Branch: Pooling Committee: Minutes and Papers 1968-1971 (ED 198)
  -    minutes and papers on redistribution of expenditure on teacher training among LEAs

9.16.3   Examining Bodies, Special Schemes, Inquiries and General Files

1.   Teachers' Registration Council: Minute Books 1902-1950 (ED 44)
  -    minutes of proceedings of Council 1902-1929, Executive Council of Royal Society of Teachers 1929-1949

2.   Teachers Joint Examination Boards Files 1927-1949 (ED 105)
  -    formation of boards; syllabuses; examination regulations; reports on examinations; examination statistics

3.   Emergency Recruitment and Training of Teachers 1943-1952 (ED 143)
  -    policy decisions on scheme and its administration; special courses for uncertified teachers

4.   Teachers: General Files 1899-1972 (ED 86)
  -    includes papers of the National Advisory Council on the Training and Supply of Teachers

5.   Teachers Branches I and II: Registered Files (R and RS Series) 1961-1978 (ED 192)
  -    continuation of ED 86 and ED 108: includes papers on recruitment, publicity, qualifications and conditions of service; NACTST; administration of training colleges

6.   Burnham Committees and Related Papers 1916-1987 (ED 108)
  -    includes papers on teachers salaries

7.   Teachers' Superannuation, Registered Files (PEN Series) 1899-1977 (ED 131)
  -    correspondence and papers on relevant legislation; wartime measures to safeguard teachers' pension rights; relationship with other public service superannuation schemes; modifications after National Insurance Act 1948

8.   Teachers' Misconduct: General Files 1904-1962 (ED 104)
-      some pieces closed for fifty or seventy-five years

9.   Elementary Education: London General Files 1870-1923 (ED 14)
-      includes papers on pupil-teachers and pupil-teacher centres

10.   Welsh Secondary Education, General Files 1900-1935 (ED 93)
-      includes papers on pupil-teachers and pupil-teacher centres

11.   Private Office Papers 1851-1935 (ED 24)
-      confidential correspondence; departmental committee papers

12.   Circulars and Administrative Memoranda 1870-1989 (ED 142)
-      includes significant circulars covering changes in teacher training

13.   Teachers' Training Inquiry (James) Committee 1971-1972 (ED 145)
-      minutes, papers and correspondence

10. INSPECTORATE

10.1   Establishment of the Inspectorate 1839-1870

In 1838, five years after the introduction of Treasury grants for school buildings, two MPs complained that the government did not know how that money was being spent because there was no inspection of schools. The following year, when the Privy Council Committee on Education was formed, inspection was made a condition of all educational grants in the first regulations issued by the committee and two inspectors were appointed. One was Seymour Tremenheere, a barrister, and the other, the Reverend John Allen, was chaplain of King's College, London. Details of the expenses they submitted for their inspections of schools are among the Treasury Board Papers, eg T 1/4745/20644.

An agreement, known as a concordat, was made with the archbishop of Canterbury in 1840 about the inspection of religious instruction in elementary schools. Under this arrangement, inspectors for Anglican schools had to be acceptable to the archbishops, who could put forward their own candidates, and inspectors had to submit their reports to the bishop of the diocese. The concordat was issued as an Order in Council 10 August 1840 (PC 2/222) and a printed copy appears in the minutes of the PCCE (ED 17/1).

Within a few years, similar agreements were made with other denominations. This meant in practice that the inspectorate was fragmented because it had to deal with the different religious bodies and was organized on a denominational rather than territorial basis. These arrangements lasted until 1870.

James Kay-Shuttleworth was appointed secretary to the PCCE and he was largely responsible for the organization and operation of the inspectorate. He saw them as autonomous professionals offering expert advice. They were individually appointed by Order in Council and became Her Majesty's Inspectors; this ensured their relative independence. The question of the continuation of this form of appointment after 1902 is debated on an establishment file (ED 23/271).

Grants were extended in 1843 and the inspectorate increased. Kay-Shuttleworth drew up instructions for inspectors: to investigate applications for building grants; to examine and report on the work of elementary schools; to make special inquiries into elementary education in certain districts. Their duties were further extended by the PCCE minutes of 1846 (ED 17/1), including responsibilities for the examination of pupil-teachers. Thereafter payment of the grant to schools depended directly on the inspector's report and this made necessary the appointment of two examiners of the reports (Temple and Lingen). Record of the appointment of further examiners in 1857 survives among the Treasury Board Papers (T 1/6062A/7530).

Matthew Arnold, son of Thomas Arnold of Rugby School, was appointed Her Majesty's Inspector of Schools in 1847 and retired in 1886. His personal file is available (ED 36/1); it contains a copy of his report on his inquiry into foreign systems of education as well as memos and personal routine letters about his work as an HMI. Further information about him can be found among the Treasury Board Papers (T 1/ 5256/11071). Other appointments and payments made during this formative period of the inspectorate will be found as follows:

1842	T 1/4745/20644
1843	T 1/4903/26523
1844	T 1/5017/24663
1845	T 1/5121/24432
1846	T 1/5202/22677
1847	T 1/5336/29735
1848	T 1/5406/23592
1849	T 1/5512/2508
1850	T 1/5610/24287
1851	T 1/5720B/26074
1853	T 1/5814A/18507
1854	T 1/5877B/15022
1857	T 1/6054B/2822
1858	T 1/6124A/9588

From 1870, papers relating to appointments to the inspectorate will be found in ED 23 (eg ED 23/410, 409, 421).

Kay-Shuttleworth suggested that, in accordance with the increase in numbers and duties of the inspectorate, the country should be divided into five districts, each with its own inspector of Anglican schools. ED 17/55-56 et seq show the HMI districts. By the time Kay-Shuttleworth retired in 1849, as a result of ill health, there were sixteen inspectors for England and Wales (twelve for Anglican schools, two for British and Wesleyan, one for Roman Catholic and one for Training Schools). There were an additional four inspectors for poor law schools.

In 1850 assistant inspectors were appointed, at half the salary, to help with the quantity of work. The assistants had to be successful elementary school headmasters, recommended and approved by the Education Department. By 1861 there were thirty-six HMIs and twenty-four assistant inspectors.

The peripatetic nature of the work meant that there were official papers to carry and keep safe. In 1858 this problem was solved through the Stationery Office by the purchase of a dispatch box and wallets for each inspector. Treasury sanction was necessary for this equipment and T 1/6124A/9588 contains a description of one of

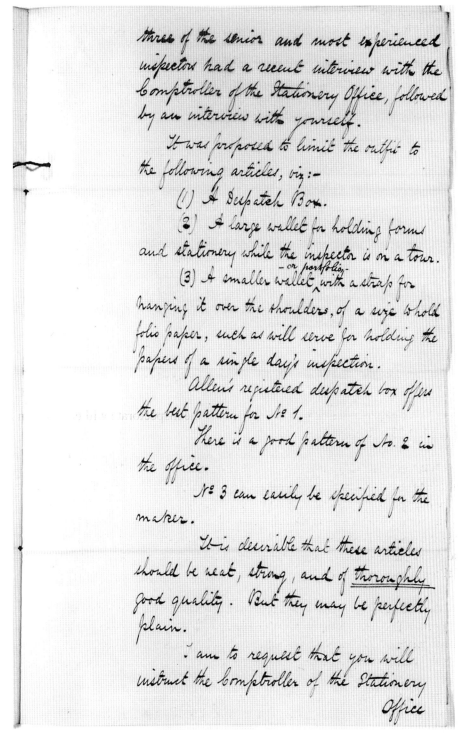

three of the senior and most experienced inspectors had a recent interview with the Comptroller of the Stationery Office, followed by an interview with yourself.

It was proposed to limit the outfit to the following articles, viz:–

(1) A Despatch Box.

(2) A large wallet for holding forms and stationery while the inspector is on a tour.

(3) A smaller wallet, – or portfolio – with a strap for hanging it over the shoulders, of a size to hold folio paper, such as will serve for holding the papers of a single day's inspection.

Allen's registered despatch box offers the best pattern for N° 1.

There is a good pattern of No. 2 in the office.

N° 3 can easily be specified for the maker.

It is desirable that these articles should be neat, strong, and of thoroughly good quality. But they may be perfectly plain.

I am to request that you will instruct the Comptroller of the Stationery Office

Figure 15
Application to the Treasury for the purchase of equipment for Her Majesty's Inspectors, March 1858 (T 1/6124A/9588)

the wallets which had to be specially designed 'with a strap for hanging it over the shoulders, of a size to hold folio paper such as will serve for holding the papers of a single day's inspection.'

The reports of these early inspectors were printed for Parliament; ED 17 includes a set of the reports from 1841 to 1899.

10.1.1 Poor Law Inspectors

In 1842 district schools became liable to HMI inspection when the PCCE began to give them grant-aid. At first poor law inspectors performed this function but from 1846 district schools were put under the supervision of the Education Department. Four HMIs were appointed to examine the condition of schools and to establish the character and qualifications of the teachers. This arrangement continued until 1863 when responsibility for the inspection of workhouse schools was transferred to the Poor Law Board (subsequently the Local Government Board); in 1904 responsibility for inspection returned to the Board of Education. Reports on district schools will be found in MH 27; those on other poor law schools attached to workhouses are in MH 12; papers of individual poor law school inspectors from 1863 is in MH 32/108-117. After 1904 information is on the surviving Poor Law School Files in ED 132. (*See also 3.7*).

10.1.2 Revised Code

The introduction of the Revised Code with its principle of payment by results caused a profound shift of emphasis in the work of the inspectorate: controlling and examining became more important than advising and encouraging. The Revised Code set out a system of examinations of individual pupils, from age six, based on Standards. The sums earned by pupils were paid to the school managers, rather than the teachers. The 'three Rs' and plain needlework were the only subjects which attracted grants; the system was gradually extended to include a greater number of subjects. Each of the Standards which pupils had to attain was set out in detail and HMIs were urged not to depart from the requirements. Pupils were grouped by Standard rather than age.

The application of the Revised Code led to friction between HMIs and teachers. Matthew Arnold called the Payment by Results system a 'game of mechanical contrivance in which the teachers will and must learn more and more how to beat us'. It was claimed by teachers that HMIs had no or very little understanding of elementary school work and yet they assessed teachers' performance and determined their salaries. Assistant inspectors redressed the balance a little but their status was lowly. Twenty-three inspectors signed a 'Grand Remonstrance' to the Lord President protesting about unjust aspersions cast upon them (HC 1862 xliii, 171-4) These related to the fact that non paying subjects (eg geography, history, art and music) suffered, that teachers' salaries were now dependent on the outcome of an inspection and that it was also difficult for an all male inspectorate to assess needlework.

10.1.3   Alteration of Reports

Robert Lowe, Vice President of the CCE, warned in 1861 that reports which did not conform to an acceptable standard would be returned to the inspector concerned with the inappropriate passages marked. He withdrew this order a year later but the practice continued. It was suspected that reports containing criticism of payment by results were being handled in this way. The subject was raised in the Commons in April 1864; Lowe resigned and an inquiry was ordered (HC 1864 ix). Lowe was cleared but the principle of the integrity of inspectors' reports was established.

10.2   After the Forster Act 1870-1902

The Newcastle Commission declared the denominational nature of the inspectorate wasteful and inefficient. Section 7(3) of the Elementary Education Act 1870 removed HMI responsibility to report on religious instruction. This meant that the concordats of the 1840s lapsed and the inspectorate could be organized territorially rather than denominationally. The country was divided into districts and the HMIs became responsible for the inspection of all schools within that district, whether voluntary or board schools. The districts were grouped into eight divisions each in the charge of a senior inspector, a newly created grade with its members taken from the most experienced inspectors. The arrangement of the reports in ED 17 reflects the inspectorate districts.

In 1882 Mundella, the new Vice-President, introduced a new category of sub-inspectors, recruited from inspectors' assistants. By the end of 1885, twenty-nine sub-inspectors had been appointed, each attached to an HMI. Inspectorate duties were recast, with greater emphasis laid on co-ordination and training. Conferences of senior inspectors and annual divisional meetings of inspectors were encouraged. ED 24/228 contains the minutes of some such conferences held before the First World War.

From its inception the Committee of Council on Education regularly issued instructions, circulars and regulations to its inspectors. These early circulars, etc were printed with the annual reports and minutes and will be found in the printed volumes in ED 17. Draft circulars to HMIs and Training Schools between 1854 and 1863 are in ED 9/15. The aim of the circulars was to keep inspectors up to date with office procedure and with current educational policy. The earlier issues of the series have suffered some destruction but they remain from 1878 in ED 22.

By the 1890s the system of payment by results was at an end: teachers had responsibility for drawing up timetables and HMI visited schools without notice. These developments were in line with the recommendations of the Cross Commission whose report contained a detailed list of the duties of HMIs (HC 1888 xxxv,xxxvi; ED 10/42). These included examining children and pupil-teachers, inspecting training colleges, monitoring school supply and advising the Department on policy and its reception countrywide.

A Senior Chief Inspector, Rev T W Sharpe, was appointed in 1890 to run the inspectorate, instead of the Chief Clerk. The Education Department argued with the Treasury in 1894 that Sharpe should be allowed to stay on beyond retirement age to assist:

> in the substitution of a more intelligent system of inspection and appraisement of educational methods, under which the Inspector becomes the adviser of school managers and teachers, and does not continue as formerly to be their judge and critic
>
> ED 23/71

10.2.1   Science and Art Department

Between 1855 and 1886 the Science and Art Department in South Kensington examined drawing in elementary schools. The Education Department took this on for the lower standards (under the Revised Code) after 1886, while the Science and Art Department retained responsibility for the work of the older pupils.

There were four South Kensington inspectors by the mid 1880s and various occasional or acting inspectors, used to supplement the knowledge of the permanent ones. There was a significant increase in the Department's work and influence, leading eventually to the pragmatic abandonment of payment by results in the late 1890s as a consequence of the mounting tide of examination scripts to be marked. Arthur Acland, Vice-President from 1892, appreciated the problem and appointed thirteen new inspectors, known as Acland's Apostles because of their zeal, and divided the country into districts each with its own qualified and experienced inspector. In 1894 Acland appointed sub-inspectors to assist and transferred some to the Education Department to inspect elementary drawing.

10.2.2   Charity Commission Inspectorate

Endowed schools were liable to inspection by the Charity Commission. In evidence to the Newcastle Commission it was stated that this was an occasional occurrence or took place only in special circumstances. The Commission had only five inspectors for every type of school and the inspectors were not particularly qualified to make educational inspections: three were barristers, one was a solicitor and the other lacked any professional training at all. The Newcastle report recommended that all endowed schools should be inspected by HMIs.

The Schools Inquiry (Taunton) Commission asked repeatedly for a proper system of inspection for endowed schools in order, at minimum, to see that the endowments were being put to proper use. The Commissioners suggested that there should be periodic inspections and examinations of schools and that each inspector should be helped by a panel of examiners and should test the schools in his district in a way which did not interfere with the normal timetables. The transfer of the work of the Endowed School Commissioners to the Charity Commissioners in 1874 was neither popular nor efficient. In the last quarter of the nineteenth century the inspections carried out on behalf of the Charity Commission were administrative rather than educational.

10.2.3   Inspectors' Reports

Copies of early inspectors' reports are within the reports of the Committee of Council on Education printed for Parliament as House of Commons Sessional Papers. ED 17 contains a set of these from 1841-1899. Other HMI reports will be found in the class of miscellanea (ED 9). ED 9/13 contains twelve files of inspectors reports on science and art day classes covering the period 1879-1905 for named schools. Confidential HMI reports (including one by Matthew Arnold) on efficiency in Roman Catholic schools in 1875 are in ED 9/14. There is a separate series of HMI reports for London elementary schools transferred to the London School Board in ED 4. Reports of inspections made for the Charity Commissioners before 1899 will be found in the Secondary Education Endowment Files (ED 27). ED 50 contains HMI reports (1872-1893) on the education of the blind in the metropolis and on the training of their teachers. ED 17/65-69 includes reports on schools for the blind and deaf in the 1890s. *For later reports see 10.3.5 and Case Study at 10.5.*

10.3   Balfour to Butler 1902-1944

The establishment of the Board of Education and the subsequent Education Act 1902 led to the reorganization of the inspectorate into elementary, secondary and technical branches each headed by a chief inspector. Papers on this reorganization will be found in ED 23/128. It was at this time that the circulars became memoranda and were issued to inspectors of elementary, secondary, technical schools, schools of art and training colleges. Copies of these memoranda continue in ED 22.

The formation of the new technical inspectorate   from the inspectors of the Science and Art Department led to the debate about retention of the title HMI (ED 23/271). The secondary inspectorate was established in 1904-1905; ED 23/130 explains the origin of the 'staff' inspectors and ED 23/340 their functions. The secondary branch evolved the full inspection method with the school as the unit of inspection.

Under the Board of Education Act 1899 the Board could inspect any school supplying secondary education and wishing to be inspected. By 1914, sixty-eight out of the 101 Headmasters Conference schools had requested and received inspection. The 1944 Act made all public schools open to inspection (*see below*).

When payment on results ended, the duties of the HMIs were altered. They no longer had to examine children and assess grants on results but could advise, help and disseminate new ideas. It took some time to break down the old hostility and distrust so that an inspection was no longer regarded as an inquisitorial visitation.

10.3.1   Women Inspectors

As early as 1873 Jane Senior, daughter of Nassau Senior, the economist, was appointed as Inspector of Workhouses and District Schools. The increased interest in girls' education and the demand for practical work for girls in schools, encouraged by the Samuelson Commission report, resulted in the introduction of cookery into the Code in 1882 and an increased emphasis on needlework. As a direct consequence Emily Jones was appointed in 1883 as the Directress of Needlework. She was not appointed HMI and was the sole female representative in the Education Department inspectorate for seven years.

The move towards specialization of the inspectorate in the 1890s led to the appointment of Mrs Harrison as an 'inspectress'. She was appointed on a temporary and experimental basis to inspect cookery and laundry work. The Cross Commission suggested that female inspectors should visit infant schools and that they could possibly be used as sub-inspectresses in large towns, although the commissioners expressed concern about practical problems 'where much travelling is required'. The Honourable Mrs Colborne succeeded Miss Jones as Directress of Needlework in 1894 and Miss Deane followed Mrs Harrison two years later. These two women were both put on the permanent staff of the Department. The Bryce Commission (the first with women members) recommended that 'duly qualified women should be chosen where there is likely to be sufficient work for them' (HC 1895 xliii; ED 12/11-12).

From 1898, the Education Department examined and granted certificates in cookery in training colleges. Two female assistant examiners were appointed to do this work. They made recommendations about training advisable in the colleges and also inspected domestic subjects in elementary schools.

Robert Morant was instrumental in founding the Women Inspectorate in 1905. Following the Physical Deterioration report (HC 1904 xxii) he saw the importance of women in elementary schools to look at infant teaching and the older girls from the 'maternity aspect'. His memo on the new post of Chief Woman Inspector emphasized the need to have a woman of real standing and prestige. This view prevailed with the appointment of the Honourable Maud Lawrence, daughter of the viceroy of India. Morant's memo also recommended the following working conditions:

> She will not herself have any fixed hours of attendance whatever, but will be quite free to be either at her own house or at a room here which we shall place at her disposal, as and when she may find the work necessitates.
>
> ED 23/152B

Their male colleagues referred to women inspectors as 'the washtub ladies' because they dealt with domestic subjects and elementary schools. The first national survey published by the inspectorate was undertaken by the women: the *Report on Children under Five Years of Age in Public Elementary Schools by Women Inspectors of the Board of Education 1905* (HC 1906 Cmnd 2726 xc).

Few women were appointed to the Secondary Inspectorate and the first woman staff inspector took up her post in 1919. There was only one woman District Inspector before 1933. Their salaries were lower than those of their male counterparts (ED 23/846). The report of the Royal Commission on the Civil Service in 1929-1931 (HC 1930-31 Cmnd 3909 x) led to all posts in the inspectorate being open to women without discrimination (ED 23/713).

10.3.2   Welsh Inspectorate

A Welsh inspectorate was formed in 1907 for Welsh elementary and secondary schools. Owen Edwards, chief inspector of the Welsh Department, built up a body of Welsh speaking inspectors (ED 23/145-148). He also submitted to the President of the Board a survey of the work of his own post (ED 24/584). A Ministry of Education publication in 1950 praised his achievements:

> the soundness of this conception is shown by its survival, unchanged in structure, and justified in practice, over a period of sixty years.

In 1951-1952 the Treasury undertook an organization and methods (O and M) report on the Welsh Department, which included HM Inspectorate in Wales. A copy is available in ED 23/933.

Reports on Welsh schools occur on the general files on Welsh education (ED 91-ED 93) and on the institution files. ED 22 contains a separate series of Welsh memoranda for the period 1907-1940; most of the later series of memoranda in ED 135 were also adopted in Wales.

10.3.3 Holmes-Morant Memorandum

In 1908 the Chief Inspector, E G A Holmes, asked his inspectors to collect information on the status, duties and efficiency of LEA inspectors. From these returns he prepared a confidential memo on local inspectors appointed by certain LEAs (E Memorandum No 21). It was very critical of these local inspectors, who were usually from the ranks of the elementary school teachers, steeped in the practices made necessary by the Elementary Code and accustomed to acrimony between teachers and HMIs. The memo was probably intended only for senior departmental officials but it was issued to the inspectorate in May 1910. A copy was leaked to the press. Sir Samuel Hoare, MP for Chelsea, took the opportunity it provided to castigate the Liberal government in March 1911 and the NUT claimed a slur had been cast on the teaching profession. The leak led to the resignation of Walter Runciman, President of the Board of Education, and the removal of R L Morant to the Insurance Commission (a move which later enabled him to become the first permanent secretary of the Ministry of Health in 1919).

The furore caused by the disclosure of the memo led to its recall from the inspectorate and its expunging from the public record. No copy exists among the set of memoranda for 1910 (ED 22/52), the number has been used for another memorandum and no discussion papers about it survive among the inspectorate papers in ED 23 or in the private office papers in ED 24. One copy is extant in the Runciman MSS RP WR 46 at Newcastle University library. The memorandum is reproduced in full in *Journal of Educational Administration and History*, vol x no 1 (1978), pp 37-40.

Most local inspectors were found in areas which had school boards before 1902. Large towns such as London, Liverpool, Manchester, Birmingham, Leeds, Sheffield, Bristol, Newcastle, Salford, Hull, Leicester and Nottingham had seventy-five out of the 123 inspectors of elementary schools, as well as numerous specialists for particular subjects.

London, where the London County Council (LCC) was unlike any other LEA, was a special case. The problems of inspection in the metropolis and their solution are outlined in a memo by F H Dale, Chief Inspector of Elementary Schools, in 1912 (ED 23/269). It seems that there was an unofficial agreement between Dale and Sir Robert Blair of the LCC that HMI did not inspect London elementary schools but rather wrote general subject reports based on sampling elementary schools. This situation was admitted within the Board of Education in 1925 (ED 23/269), had broken down when discussed by Lord Stanhope and representatives from the LCC in 1937 and was not remedied until the intervention of R A Butler in 1943 (ED 23/667).

Various changes were made in the organization of the inspectorate following the Education Act 1921 and the Hadow report. Information about this reorganization will be found in ED 23/341.

10.3.4   Panel System

After 1933 the Panel System began: groups of inspectors collected information on the teaching of a particular subject (ED 23/712). ED 158 contains records of twenty-five main panels, various sub-panels and committees. The papers of some panels and sub-panels have not survived.

The panel system was reconstituted in 1945 and consisted of eighty panels. The panels were to study educational developments and research, to collect and disseminate information to the inspectorate and beyond, to organize in-service training for teachers, to produce pamphlets and other publications and to provide advice for the Ministry. ED 176 contains minutes and reports of the Central Panel (1944-1964), which co-ordinated the activities of all the other panels and maintained links with the Information and External Relations Branch (papers in ED 121).

10.3.5   Inspectors' Reports

After 1899, abstracts of inspectors' reports are in the appropriate class of institution file (*see 10.5*). ED 109 contains a master set of inspection reports on secondary schools and notes of meetings between the governing body and the inspectors at the time of the inspection. It also includes reports made by specialist inspectors, eg replies to the 1932 survey into the health of schoolchildren. Reports on further education establishments are in ED 114 and on teacher training colleges in ED 115.

10.4   Post-War Inspectorate

The wartime debate on educational reconstruction, the Norwood Report and the McNair Report affected the inspectorate. The unofficial arrangement that HMIs did not inspect London schools was ended by R A Butler, the President of the Board of Education (ED 23/667, *see above 10.3.3*). Martin Roseveare, the Chief Inspector, undertook a thorough reorganization of the inspectorate in the wake of the new Education Act 1944. Roseveare was convinced that:

> we must allow for getting there and for relieving the HMI to <u>think</u>, instead of killing him with donkey work.
>
> ED 23/714

He recommended that the separate elementary, secondary and technical branches be discontinued, the number of grades reduced, a separate women inspectorate disbanded and that assistant inspectors should become full HMIs. His reorganization was introduced on 1 April 1945 and created a unified service with six Chief Inspectors under a Senior Chief Inspector (ED 23/714 and 838).

HMI contributed to the physical side of reconstruction, with a full-time HMI attached to the Architects and Buildings Branch (*see chapter 12*). The inspectorate was also involved in the debate about external examinations and the curriculum in secondary schools (*see chapter 11*).

The Report from the Select Committee on Education and Science (Her Majesty's Inspectorate, HC 1967-8i Cmnd 3860) recommended that emphasis be laid on consultancy, advice and informal visits rather than upon formal inspections . Two working groups were set up 1969-1970 on HMI: one, under T R (later Sir Toby) Weaver reviewed the working of the HMI in FE; the other looked at the effects on the inspectorate of the Fulton Report on the civil service (The Civil Service: Report of the Committee, chaired by Lord J S Fulton of Falmer, HC 1967-8 xviii Cmnd 3638). The work of the HMI featured in the DES produced 'Yellow Book', *School Education in England: Problems and Initiatives,* 1976:

> HM Inspectorate is without doubt the most powerful single agency to influence what goes on in schools both in kind and in standard.

10.4.1 Inspectorate Reports

Post-1944, the special series of inspectorate reports continue for secondary schools in ED 109 and for teacher training colleges in ED 115. ED 114 contains reports on further education institutes up to 1963, with additional reports in ED 149, ED 196 and ED 197. Other new series of reports began after the Education Act 1944: on primary schools in ED 156, on independent schools in ED 172 (closed for fifty years), on special education in ED 195 and on school meals in ED 194 (including reports on the nutritional value of meals, kitchens, utensils and supervision of kitchen staff and children). A new series of inspectorate memoranda was opened in 1941 and is in ED 135. Other collected special reports occur in ED 77, many of them on free places (ED77/17-137). Other reports by HMI into examinations for free places are in ED 110. (*See also Case Study at 10.5.*)

10.4.2 Publications

A new Inspectors' Bulletin was introduced in 1949 (ED 23/828 and 829) as a revival of a pre-war information pamphlet which has not survived. There were three issues a year and it was a means of informing HMI of panel developments and a vehicle for views of individual inspectors. A broad spectrum of subjects was covered: conferences, foreign visits and educational systems, curriculum changes and teaching methods. Copies of the Bulletin are in ED 179.

The Information Service was launched by the Ministry of Education in 1959. It aimed to keep HMI up to date on current educational thought. Topics covered in the resulting

Information Series included curriculum development, examinations and school organization. Later the scope was broadened to include theoretical and policy matters.

The following year the Information Gazette was produced to provide factual background information for HMI, useful in their daily work. It gave news of conferences, various projects, staff activities, panel work, book reviews and bibliographies. After sixteen years, in 1976, the Gazette was discontinued and more use made of the Information Series and Personal Notes. The latter have not survived but copies of both the Gazette and Information Series are available in ED 179.

HMI together with the Library Association and the School Library Association formed the Tripartite Committee which met on an ad hoc basis between 1950 and 1962 to discuss matters relating to libraries and books. In 1967 an abortive attempt was made to revive the committee, which was never formally dissolved, to act as a steering group for the co-operation exercise with the Public Library service and School Libraries. The minutes, papers and correspondence of the Tripartite Committee are in ED 211.

10.5 Case Study of the work of an HMI and the development, format and content of HMI reports

WHEREABOUTS OF HMI REPORTS FOR ELEMENTARY/PRIMARY AND SECONDARY SCHOOLS			
Date	**Elementary/ Primary Schools**	**Endowed Secondary Schools**	**LEA Secondary Schools after 1902**
1840-1899	ED 17 Annual Reports ED 21 School Files ED 2 Parish Files	ED 35 Institution Files ED 27 Endowment Files	
1900-1944	ED 21 School Files ED 2 Parish Files	ED 109 HMI Reports ED 35 Institution Files	ED 109 HMI Reports ED 35 Institution Files

Date	Elementary	Endowed	LEA
post 1944	ED 156 HMI Reports ED 161 Digest Files ED 185 School History Sheets	ED 109 HMI Reports ED 162 Digest Files	ED 109 HMI Reports ED 162 Digest Files

10.5.1   Day in the life of a typical HMI in the 1870s

EM Sneyd-Kinnersley was appointed HMI in rural Norfolk during the early 1870s, just after the Forster Education Act. After three years he moved to Chester and continued to inspect schools in the Chester District for a further twenty-five years. When he retired, he wrote an autobiography in which he described a typical day's work:

> I . . . usually went off on the Monday morning to one of the outlying settlements and made that a centre for 5 days. As a rule I got to school about 10 with a margin. The children did nothing beyond the rudiments. I finished the work by 11.45, went to the Rectory, and inspected the garden, or played croquet with the Rector's daughters; had a noble lunch; drove back to my inn, marked the school papers, wrote the Report and posted it . . .

Inspectors completed a weekly diary showing daily employment and daily expenditure on travelling. Sneyd-Kinnersley records that in two autumn weeks in Norfolk he inspected 606 children and incurred travelling expenses of £11. Thirty years later in Manchester he inspected 600 children in a single department in a school and his travelling expenses were 2d.

Once the reports were written they were sent in full to the Education Department and seen by examiners. If they were approved then they were forwarded to the school. The manuscript originals do not survive among the records of the PCCE or the Education Department before 1870. Some individual reports may be found on the school files (ED 21) or occasionally among the parish files (ED 2) for the latter part of the nineteenth century.

It has proved impossible to find any of Sneyd-Kinnersley's full reports on individual schools among the records of the Education Department. Some of his general reports as district inspector for Chester are printed among the annual reports for Parliament (ED 17) either in full (eg ED 17/49 for 1878) or in extract as quoted by his divisional inspector in the printed report (eg ED 17/55 for 1884 and ED 17/69 for 1898). No reports of school inspection for Lower Bebington in Cheshire, the school chosen in the case study at 3.14, written by Sneyd-Kinnersley have been found.

10.5.2   HMI Reports 1840-1899 - Bebington National School

Between 1840 and 1899 HMI reports were printed for Parliament as part of the annual report of the Education Department and rarely contain detailed reports for individual schools. There are usually general reports for the counties for which a district or divisional inspector was responsible. Before 1870 they are arranged by religious affiliation of the school and contain brief tabulated information relating to the schools visited during the year; it was impossible for HMI to visit each school every year. After 1870, the printed general divisional reports contain extracts from the reports made by the contributing district HMI and sometimes quote names of individual schools.

The following information for Bebington National School has been found among the printed reports:

ED 17/8 Abstract of a report by Rev Moseley of inspection 5 May 1845

> Erected, by the aid of a Treasury grant, at a cost of £200, exclusive of the master's house. The site was given by Sir P Stanley. I found 150 children assembled in the boys', girls' and infants' school, which number they were built to contain. I was not invited to inspect the school. There is an ancient endowment of 20 acres of land, the rent of which is paid to a superannuated schoolmaster. The land, by reason of its proximity to the rising town of Birkenhead, is of great value.

ED 17/10 Abstract of a report by Rev Muirhead-Mitchell of inspection 13 August 1847

> Rooms inconveniently fitted up. Cold stone floor. Master trained at Chester. School needs improvement. There is an endowment of 20 acres of land about to become valuable. It would be advisable to rebuild the rooms. The infants are under a girl of 15, and not very well managed. There is a want of maps, pictures, etc., at present. The funds are very small.

ED 17/11 Abstract of a report by Rev Muirhead-Mitchell of inspection 23 January 1849

> School improved; in three classes. Discipline fair, and instruction good. The master teaches well, but should cultivate a better manner. There is a want of books, maps and apparatus. The premises of the school are much confined, and the fittings awkward. The house does not belong to the school, though attached to the room. The master deserves his augmentation.

ED 17/19 Abstract of Report by Rev Norris of inspection 18 August 1853

> Boys school
>
> Buildings poor, stone floor; separate rooms for boys and girls and class-room for infants; teachers residence. Wall desks. Playground common to boys

and girls. Books, a few of the Dublin reading-books, but insufficient. Organisation, boys in four classes under Mr Colbeck. Discipline and instruction defective.

Girls school

Wall desks. Organisation, girls in four classes, under Miss Firth. Discipline fair, apparently. This school had a small building grant from the Lords of the Treasury eighteen years ago. It is endowed with twenty-six acres of ground, which are likely to become valuable. The children appeared to have learned their lessons memoriter, without much exercise of the understanding. They pay from 4d to 1°d per week

10.5.3   Extracts from HMI Sneyd-Kinnersley's reports as reproduced in printed annual reports

ED 17/49 General HMI report on Chester District by HMI E M Sneyd-Kinnersley 1878

> . . . Private adventure schools paralysing the efforts of school boards and school attendance committees, and demoralising parents and children by the shelter they afford against the law . . .

ED 17/55 HMI Blandford quotes from Sneyd-Kinnersley's report on the work of the school attendance committee and on achievements in the various standards in schools in the Chester District:

> In the standard work there has been a material improvement since the introduction of the New Code, not so much in the accuracy as in the style of the work; and the intelligence of the methods. We are rapidly getting rid of monotonous reading, even in the infants' schools. We get good writing as well as good spelling in a condition for a pass; we are making vigorous war against counting on fingers, though at present with partial success . . .

ED 17/69 General report on the North Central Division by HMI Parez in 1895 includes a lengthy extract from Sneyd-Kinnersley's general report on his district. The local HMI speaks particularly highly of the Port Sunlight schools and the variability of teaching in his area:

> . . . to the Sunlight Soap Company at least some recognition is due of their enterprise and liberality. . . . Messrs Lever, when building a small town for their workpeople, did not shrink from the moral claims on them, and have erected costly schools in the middle of their model village, which they support with great liberality . . .

> . . . Why do not children come to school? . . . some because the school is so uncomfortable or so badly taught that they shrink from the misery and waste of time . . . "They don't larn nothing", was the defence of a village when accused of wholesale truancy . . .

. . . I have one infant school where every child is taught to open his lower jaw, remembering that the upper jaw is a fixture, and there the children can both read and sing. But the school is unique . . .

10.5.4   HMI work post-1870 as reflected in a Parish File (ED 2)

The Parish File for Bebington (ED 2/39) contains an inspector's report on the township of Lower Bebington carried out in 1872 in accordance with the Forster Act 1870. It confirms that there are two schools in the area: Bebington National C of E and New Ferry C of E. Correspondence from 1906 demonstrates the power exercised by local men of influence over schools they supported financially.

Letter from HMI F Howard October 1906 (spelling and abbreviations as in the original)

I think the Bd should know of trouble which is brewing.

Mr Lever M.P. is lord paramount in Port Sunlight. There are 2 schools and the Foundation Managers are representatives of the settlement committee not of the Parish Council of Bebington in which civil parish the model village is situate.

A few months ago Mr Lever offered to present to the schools of Port Sunlight certain framed pictures about 5 feet in length of statuary (Venus, Apollo etc) which he had brought from Italy on condition that he was put to no expense for hanging. The LEA Subctee for that portion of Cheshire decided to accept the pictures <u>if HMI would say that they were suitable for hanging in an elementary school.</u>

I referred the matter to my then Divisional I Mr Kynnersley [*sic*] who expressed the opinion that according to my description the pictures were not suitable for a Mixed School because in such cases "Puris omnia pura" should read "Pueris omnia impura".

I accompanied the Secty of the Subctee to the 2 schools and pointed out 2 pictures which I thought might be of direct use for educational purposes because the figures represented were clothed .

The Secty thought he could arrange matters without further trouble & ∴ nothing was put in writing. After he had interviewed Mr Lever's representative a letter came setting out Mr Lever's own views which of course may be embodied in "Puris omnia pura".

I declined to say anything beyond what I had said before and I suggested that the question be referred to the LEA itself. But when Mr Lever's letter and my own were read at the meeting of the Subctee the County Inspector took the same view as myself. The S.C. then reaffirmed "its decision <u>not</u> to accept the pictures in question with exception of two to which objection was not raised by HMI" This resolution was accepted by the LEA without challenge.

Notwithstanding all this Mr Lever has visited the schools - has personally supervised the hanging of the pictures & has dared the teachers to remove them and threatens to close the schools if the LEA carries out its resolution.

I do not think the LEA will alter its resolution but I expect that it will not give instructions to remove the pictures. If it does Mr Lever will fight.

Am I justified in saying that I advised the LEA to the best of my ability and I still think that when "life-size" photos of statuary of this particular type are likely to be misunderstood by children in a Mixed School but if the LEA considers that the moral instruction of the children will in no sense be interfered with by the constant exhibition of these and other pictures of a like character the B. of E. will not interfere as far as its grants to the 2 schools are concerned?

The matter was referred to the Chief Inspector EGA Holmes and he agreed with HMI Howard that the matter should be dropped.

In 1908 HMI Howard produced a general report on the work of schools in the Administrative Sub District of Bebington. It is a detailed piece of work citing examples from the several schools in the district and was seen by the Board of Education as a model of its kind. His main criticism of the existing system is 'overgrouping of classes' ie where children remain in the same standard for more than one year and often repeat work, particularly when there are insufficient teachers for one per standard. He also argues 'for the adoption of a lightened curriculum and the reintroduction of more individual work by children'.

10.5.5   HMI reports on School Files (ED 21)

ED 21/24402 Lower Bebington C of E Boys 169

Inspection 9th June 1920 by HMI J Winn.

At this period the reports are on pre-printed pages written in manuscript and are usually a précis of a longer report written by the HMI directly responsible but reduced to the essentials by his senior HMI for the Board of Education. The full report does not survive on the school file. A copy would have been sent to the school and to the LEA. The reports are designed to occupy no more than one side of the paper, on the obverse are 'Observations to Board and LEA and Managers'.

> eg
> . . . Their attainments in arithmetic are distinctly above the average . . . The prose and poetry chosen for Literature study should to a greater extent be such as appeal to the natural taste of a boy . . .

The reverse is headed 'Observations not necessarily for communication to Authority or Managers'. This section is rarely completed but in this instance HMI Winn has written:

There has been 'trouble' at this site & the LEA asked me for a Report

ED 21/24402 Bebington and Bromborough, Bebington CE 34A

Inspection 19-23 Jan & 7,8 March 1923 by HMI Harding.

Girls

. . . In Cl 1 (stds V to VII) exceptionally good work is done in both mental and written arithmetic. The standard of English is also high. The encouragement given to the girls to read and appreciate good literature has had marked effect on the quality of the composition . . .

Boys

. . . Substantial progress has been made in this Department since the Report of June 1920. The schemes of work have been augmented; the Headmaster's terminal examinations are now wider in scope and his written criticisms have been rendered stimulating and helpful . . .

Infants

. . . in Cl 2, possibly more interesting and not less rapid development would be made if the teacher considered more carefully the grading of the various stages in the individual work and also the advisability of keeping simple records showing individual progress . . .

Précis written and signed by HMI McInnes.

ED 21/24402 Bebington & Bromborough, Bebington CE Boys'

Inspected by HMI G F Dakin on 29 June 1927 written and signed by HMI J MacInnes.

Some of the recommendations made in the report of March, 1923 have been carried out, but the most important, that of giving more training in habits of private study in the Senior Class, has not been adequately followed . . .

In order to lessen the distraction caused by the nearness of Classes 1 and 2 to each other in the main room, it would be well if they were separated by some form of screen or partition . . .

ED 21/24402 Bebington and Bromborough, Bebington CE Girls' 34A

Inspection by HMI Dakin 31 October 1927, report written by HMI MacInnes (1p).

The number on the roll is 97, and the number for which accommodation is recognized is 88. The average attendance . . . was 95. Classes 1 & 2 are

especially inconvenienced by this pressure on the accommodation as they are
taught undivided from one another in the main room . . .

A large proportion of the girls get Practical Instruction at the local Domestic
Centres, but at present the general school curriculum is academic in character,
and as suggested at the visit, needs to be given a more practical bias . . .

The Board wants to take up the accommodation issue with the LEA but they refer to
HMI MacInnes.

This is certainly a bad case of overcrowding . . . At the same time the area
is one which presents peculiar local difficulties and before taking any action
in this isolated case I should be glad to have your views.

The HMI's views are not recorded on the surviving papers on the file.

The infants were inspected at the same time by HMI Dakin, as reported by HMI
MacInnes (1p).

. . . Steady progress is being made in the formal subjects in both classes. The
teacher of class 2 should allow the children who are better mentally endowed
to proceed at a faster pace . . .

ED 21/24402 Lower Bebington CE 34A

Inspection by HMI G F Dakin 23 November 1931, written and signed HMI J MacInnes
(3pp).

The schools in this district were reorganized in 1929 and Lower Bebington CE became
a mixed school for juniors and infants. The classes were difficult to organize because
of the irregular sizes of the rooms. The infants department number 116, taught in
classes of 50 and 66.

. . . The organisation would be improved if the wide age ranges which exist
in each of the classes were reduced by making future promotions on an age
basis . . . No Time Table has been made to suit the school as it is now
constituted, and one should be drawn up without delay . . . Considering the
conditions in which the children are taught very fair progress is being made
in the formal work in classes 1-5, but there are backward sections in each
group with whom the teachers should endeavour to deal more effectively . . .

The notes on the reverse which are not for the Authority or Managers indicate some
progress in staffing:

In consequence of representations made at this visit, an additional teacher
has been appointed for the Infants.

ED 21/47962 Bebington C of E 35A

Inspection by HMI Miss Brindley & HMI G C Allen on 8 and 9 June 1938, written and reported by HMI Stringer (1p).

It seems that nothing has been done about the accommodation, although numbers are down from 289 to 217

> . . . even with the present numbers, the school is still poorly housed, two of the classrooms being particularly small and illventilated for the classes which they contain . . .

The format of HMI reports changes after the Education Act 1944. It seems that they are typed in full on a standard form. The name of the inspector is inserted in manuscript on the title page and the standard form makes it clear that the report is confidential, may only be published in full and that copyright lies with HMSO.

10.5.6   HMI reports post 1944

10.5.6.1 ED 156/5 Bebington C of E School Cheshire

Report by HMI W W French of inspection 1 & 2 November 1951.

Mr French notes particular problems with the state of the toilets. A scullery has been installed in part of the washroom to help with the provision of meals but the whole arrangement seems both unsatisfactory and insanitary. Problems with accommodation remain; three of the seven classes are housed in one room and the Head Mistress uses a space screened off from the rest of the school as her office. The school has recently been decorated and has a large playground. He concludes

> It is possible that under the Local Education Authority's Development Plan this school will be closed and it would be unreasonable to suggest major alterations which might only be temporary. Improvement of the sanitary and washing arrangements and proper partitioning of the big room are the most urgent of the School's many needs.

After pointing out the deficiencies in certain aspects of the work set and produced, and noting that the Head and four of the teachers are new, the inspector comments:

> . . . Though most of the new teachers show plenty of promise they are necessarily lacking in experience. Two of the other teachers are energetically applying methods to which they have become accustomed over long years, but whatever the merits of these methods may be they do not harmonise with those attempted in other classes.

Another copy of this report is on the school digest file for Bebington (ED 161/1601).

10.5.7   Inspectors' Reports on Secondary Schools

This section uses examples from Kendrick Girls' School, the case study for a secondary school at 4.10.

HMI REPORTS ON KENDRICK GIRLS' SCHOOL		
Institution/Digest Files	**Dates**	**Inspectorate Reports**
ED 35/76	1903	ED 109/126
ED 35/76	1905	
ED 35/76	1906	
ED 35/76	1907	
ED 35/76	1908	ED 109/127
ED 35/76	1914	ED 109/128
ED 35/76	1918	
	1923	ED 109/129
	1934	ED 109/130
	1951	ED 109/8629
ED 162/138	1961	ED 109/9572

The endowment files in ED 27 contain no reports of inspections on Kendrick Girls' School carried out by inspectors for the Charity Commissioners. Confidential information for the use of the inspectorate alone is regularly recorded in square brackets in the reports on secondary schools. The remarks are not intended to be included in the final version. Reports on the school begin in 1903 with a full or special inspection in response to an application by the governors for recognition under the secondary school regulations. There is a copy of that report on both the institution file (ED 35/76) and among the inspectorate reports (ED 109/126).

Three more minor reports follow on the school file (ED 35/76) for 1905, 1906 and 1907. Their format is of a standard form with pre-printed questions to be answered by an inspector and their purpose is to satisfy the Board of Education that the school is adhering to the appropriate regulations and is correctly in receipt of grant. For the first of these reports in 1905 the school had been visited three times during the year by HMI Theodosius. For the second, the same HMI had visited twice and for the third report one visit had sufficed and no general remarks were made at the end by HMI Stephens because

> This school is to receive a Full Inspection next term, and I do not think it is desirable to anticipate the FI report.

Two copies of the full inspection in March 1908 are available (ED 35/76 and ED 109/127), together with a synopsis of the report listing excellences and defects (including criticisms of the premises and certain teaching staff). The third full inspection took place in October 1914 (copies in ED 35/76 and ED 109/128).

In 1918 a separate report on music in the school was carried out by HMI Somervell, a music specialist, and is included on the institution file (ED 35/76). The report is double-sided and in manuscript and quite critical. The accompanying notes record that a copy was sent to the Head Mistress.

There are no more HMI reports for Kendrick Girls' School in ED 35. The only remaining source for the next three full inspection reports is ED 109. That class contains copies of the full inspection of 1923 (ED 109/129 the first printed report on the school) with remarks about the temperament of the Head Mistress in the confidential section in square brackets. The full inspection undertaken in June 1934 is in ED 109/130 and includes a copy of the notes on the conference on the report held with the governing body. Similarly, the HMI report for May 1951 (ED 109/8629) also includes a note on the discussion with the governing body but not any remarks in square brackets. The March 1961 HMI report is available both in the inspectorate series (ED 109/9572) and on the school digest file (ED 162/138).

10.6   List of Classes

Inspectorate papers will be found on many classes of school file, especially before 1939. Full inspection reports on individual schools are now open to public inspection after thirty years.

10.6.1   Primary Schools

1.   Inspectorate: Reports on Primary Institutions 1946-1970 (ED 156)
    -    reports of inspections on maintained primary schools

2.   Inspectorate: Panels 1933-1975 (ED 158)
    -    papers of primary education committee

10.6.2 Secondary Schools

1. Reports on Secondary Institutions 1900-1971 (ED 109)
    -   reports of full inspections; specialist reports

10.6.3 Further Education

1. Inspectorate: Reports on Institutes of Further Education 1909-1965 (ED 114)
    -   reports on FE institutes; surveys of FE provision in specific areas

2. Inspectorate: Reports on Youth Welfare 1946-1965 (ED 149)
    -   includes reports on youth clubs, day continuation schools, institutions of further education, evening institutes, adult education centres

3. Inspectorate:Reports on Adult Education 1946-1965 (ED 196)
    -   includes reports on evening institutes, adult education centres and colleges

4. Inspectorate: Reports on Independent Further Education Institutions 1957-1964 (ED 197)
    -   reports on independent institutions offering FE; includes private language schools

10.6.4 Private Schools

1. Inspectorate: Reports on Independent Schools 1938-1969 (ED 172)

10.6.5 Teacher Training Colleges

1. Inspectorate: Reports on Teacher Training Colleges 1907-1959 (ED 115)
    -   reports on teacher training colleges and universities with similar courses

10.6.6 Special Services

1. Inspectorate: Reports on Special Education Establishments 1947-1969 (ED 195)
    -   reports on special education establishments; area surveys

2. Inspectorate: Reports and Surveys on School Meals Service 1954-1965 (ED 194)
    -   printed reports on school meals service within each LEA; copies of minutes of meetings between inspectors and LEAs

10.6.7   Miscellaneous and General

1.   Miscellanea 1839-1906 (ED 9)
-   includes inspectorate reports

2.   Committee of the Privy Council on Education, Minutes and Reports 1839-1899 (ED 17)
-   includes annual reports of inspectors of schools and teacher training colleges

3.   Inspectorate Memoranda 1878-1941 (ED 22)
-   copies of circulars and memoranda issued to HMIs

4.   Inspectorate Memoranda, New Series 1941-1982 (ED 135)

5.   Inspectorate: Special Reports 1909-1970 (ED 77)
-   reports on diverse subjects, including free places

6.   Fees and Special Places: Local Education Authorities Files 1932-1946 (ED 110)
-   includes reports on free (special) place examinations

7.   Inspectorate: Central Panel 1944-1964 (ED 176)
-   reports co-ordinating work of 80 separate subject panels, etc

8.   HM Inspectorate: Registered Files   (INS Series) 1964-1970   (ED 213)
-   selection of papers collected for their common interest to HMIs, relating to organization, specific subject areas or types of pupil

11. CURRICULA AND EXAMINATIONS

11.1 Elementary Curriculum to 1944

In the early nineteenth century the elementary curriculum was largely controlled by the religious bodies which ran the schools. Later, however, if a school wanted government money it had to meet minimum requirements and standards. The introduction of grants and inspection placed pressure on the voluntary schools with regard to their curricula. The inspectors advised and cajoled, and the grants for apparatus and books introduced in the 1840s encouraged the teaching of secular subjects as did the pupil teacher system of 1846 (underwritten with government money) and the introduction of capitation grants in the 1850s. The inspectors' reports in ED 17 reflect what was taught in the voluntary schools.

The report of the Newcastle Commission (T 74/1-2; HC 1861 xxi) revealed that teachers were neglecting certain subjects and that only half the elementary schools were being inspected. The result was the introduction of the system of payment by results, which laid down a very explicit curriculum to be followed in elementary schools - reading, writing and arithmetic, with plain needlework for girls. Initially, these were the only subjects to attract grants. Each 'standard' a pupil had to attain was set out in detail. School grants were determined no longer by teacher qualifications but by attendance and by the results of an annual examination of all children on the narrowly prescribed curriculum. Robert Lowe, vice president of the Education Department, and the man responsible for the revised code said:

> Teachers desiring to criticise the Code were as impertinent as chickens wishing
> to decide the sauce in which they would be served.

The content of the Code and hence the elementary curriculum was gradually enriched during the nineteenth century, particularly after the Education Act 1870. This development can be traced through the *Codes of Regulations* which were published for Parliament; copies are available in ED 17. Information about the provision of religious instruction after 1870 will be found on the LEA files ED 16 and ED 18.

The first director of the Office of Special Inquiries and Reports, Michael Sadler, instigated an exhaustive survey of the curriculum. Between 1897 and 1914 he supervized the publication of twenty-eight volumes of *Special Reports on Educational Subjects*, covering all aspects of the curriculum. These are also known as the 'Sadler Reports'. They were published by HMSO and copies are held at the Department for Education and Employment Information Bureau (*see under Useful Addresses*) and in many large reference libraries.

The Cockerton Judgment (*see chapter 2.3*) continued the debate on what could be taught in elementary schools and sharpened the distinction between the elementary and post-elementary curricula. ED 14/41 and ED 14/102-104 contain details of the curricula being followed in higher elementary schools in the capital at this time. The elementary code of 1904 ensured that there would be no advanced work in elementary schools. However, central control of the curriculum for these schools was relaxed in 1926 when the *Code of Regulations* became a *Handbook of Suggestions.*

Information about what was being taught in London elementary schools in the first decade of this century will be found in the London General Files: ED 14/95 includes inspectors' reports on the teaching of English, science (including nature study and gardening), mathematics, geography, history and needlework. ED 11 code 9 lists some surviving policy papers of the Board of Education on elementary school curricula for this period (ED 11/246, 113, 247) . It also contains policy information about specific subjects: religious instruction, domestic subjects, infant care and management, music, spelling and needlework. Files on special subjects are listed in ED 11 code 8/6. ED 106 contains information about the teaching of religious instruction in elementary schools in accordance with the provisions of the Education Act 1921. ED 24 Code 39 includes some information on the RE curriculum and Code 50 contains some papers on moral instruction and music as well as files on methods of instruction.

11.2   Secondary Curriculum to 1944

The endowed grammar schools gradually broadened their curricula during the nineteenth century. Many had never been confined to classical studies by their foundation statutes; others took advantage of the Eldon Judgment of 1805 and charged fees for subjects beyond those for which they were endowed. The Charity Commissioners took the view that so long as the main purpose of teaching the classics was maintained then other subjects could be added. Some schools obtained the right to introduce non-classical subjects by private Act of Parliament. The work of the Taunton Commission (*see chapter 4.2.2*) had little effect on the curricula independence of the endowed grammar schools. The secondary schools set up after the Education Act 1902 often modelled their courses on those of the established grammar schools.

In 1913 the Board of Education issued Circular 826 'Memorandum on Teaching and Organisation in Secondary Schools' which refers to some curricula differences between male and female pupils; ED 12/452 contains a copy. The Consultative Committee considered secondary education (*see chapter 4.5*). In 1923 it reported on the differentiation of curricula between the sexes; some correspondence and comments on the recommendations are available in ED 12/452. The Spens report advocated a subject arrangement for the secondary curriculum (ED 10/151-153, 221-222; ED 12/530; ED 136/131).

Information about courses in secondary schools will be found on the school files in ED 35, among the inspectors reports in ED 109 and in the LEA schemes files in ED

120. Policy papers on the secondary school curriculum after 1902 are in ED 12 code 4/1 for general matters and 4/2 for particular subjects, ie agriculture, religious instruction, domestic science, geometry and algebra, commercial subjects, geography, handicraft, music, speech training, languages, art and architecture, history, PE, science, civics, engineering, natural history, biology, nursing and aeronautics.

11.3   Development of the examination system

The use of written examinations as a means of selection and qualification grew during the nineteenth century: competitive examinations were introduced in 1870 as a means of entry to senior grades in the civil service; Oxford and Cambridge reformed their examination systems and demanded evidence that certain standards had been attained by prospective undergraduates; examinations replaced patronage for entry to the professions. These developments had an effect on established grammar schools.

The Oxford and Cambridge 'Locals' began in 1858. These were 'local' examinations organized by the universities and taken by pupils from both endowed and private schools. The Oxford and Cambridge Joint Board examinations started in 1874 first with a higher certificate for candidates of eighteen plus. Ten years later a lower certificate was introduced for younger pupils and in 1905 a school certificate for sixteen and seventeen year olds.

Matriculation regulations had been in place for intending undergraduates of London University since 1839 but by the end of the century they were being used increasingly by secondary schools and employers as school-leaving qualifications. Other universities introduced similar regulations.

11.4   Secondary Schools Examination Council

Both the Taunton Commission (1868) and the Bryce Commission (1895) had recommended central control of examinations. In 1904 the Board of Education discussed a system for school certificates (ED 24/184). The matter was referred to the Consultative Committee, which reported in 1911 (ED 24/212, 220, 1634). Its recommendations were accepted in 1917.

Universities were designated as responsible bodies for conducting external examinations and the Secondary Schools Examination Council (SSEC) was established with representatives from universities, LEAs and the teaching profession. Information on the constitution, establishment of and appointments to the Council is in ED 12/246, 259, 481-484; ED 24/1243-1245; ED 136/642. Two standard examinations were recognized: School Certificate at sixteen and Higher School Certificate at eighteen. The Board of Education declared that the 'examination should follow the curriculum and not determine it'. The SSEC had to co-ordinate the school

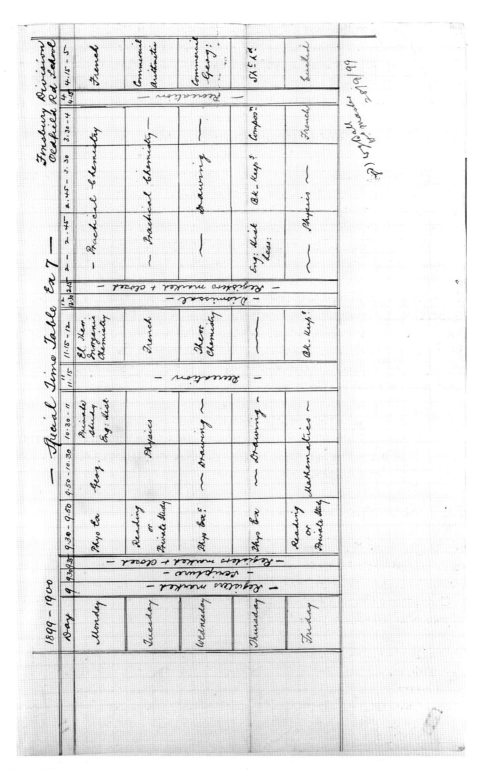

Figure 16
A timetable for a higher grade school, c1900 (ED 14/41)

certificate examinations and to maintain nationally respected standards. Its investigations of and reports on the working of these examinations are in ED 12/248, 250-251, 253-257. Other working papers are in ED 12/531-532.

After the Norwood report (*see below 11.6*), the SSEC was re-formed; ED 136/681 contains information about the council's reaction to that report. Papers relating to the reconstitution of the SSEC and appointments to it are in ED 136/790-794, with subsequent working papers in ED 147/133-8, 212-326, 1326-1343 and EJ 2/1, 2-6.

11.5   Free Places and Scholarships

The London School Board files include information about the provision of free places in elementary schools in Westminster at the end of the nineteenth century (ED 14/86). ED 16 also contains some papers on the provision of free elementary school places under the Education Act 1891. The Education (Administrative Provisions) Act 1907 introduced the free place scholarship system to give promising children from elementary schools the opportunity of admission to secondary school. Grant-aided secondary schools were allowed to admit free place scholars (not less than twenty-five per cent of the previous year's total intake) who had spent at least the last two years at a public elementary school. The school received payment per head for each scholar (ED 12/119,125, 327; ED 24 code 48/3). ED 107 and ED 63 contain LEA schemes for the payment of allowances to elementary school children qualifying for these places. ED 11/155 and 156 record discussions between the Board of Education and the Treasury on the payment of the maintenance grants. The secondary school files (ED 35), the LEA files on secondary education (ED 53) and the inspectorate special reports (ED 77) also contain some papers on the administration of the free place scheme. ED 93/1-2,7 relate to free places in Welsh secondary schools.

A departmental committee on scholarships and free places in 1920 (ED 12/434) led to restrictions being imposed on the scheme in 1922-1923; information about protests survives in ED 12/327, 348-349. Further limitations were imposed after the financial crisis of 1931; the free place system was replaced by special places for which a means tested scale of fees was introduced. ED 12 contains the policy papers on the revised scheme, together with the complaints about it (ED 12/352-367) as well as papers on aid to pupils between 1919 and 1935 (ED 12/262-269) and files on scholarship provision from 1936-1945 (ED 12/486-487). LEA files on the administration of the revised scheme are in ED 110 and ED 55. ED 110 also contains HMI reports on the free/special place examinations. Other HMI reports on free places between 1922 and 1939 are in ED 77/17-137, arranged by county. Further policy papers on the schemes are in ED 24 Code 48/3.

The Education Act 1944 extended the provision of free education to all maintained secondary schools and free or assisted places were reserved solely for direct grant grammar schools. ED 59 and ED 53 contain the earlier LEA files on the administration of grants to non-provided secondary schools. Further information about fees and special places for the period 1945-1955 is in ED 147/142-146,187.

11.5.1   State Scholarships and other Awards

The State Scholarship Scheme was introduced in 1920 for 200 state secondary school pupils. In assessing the value of individual awards, the Board of Education was guided by university committees, which were a continuation of the local advisory committees associated with the scheme for the higher education of ex-service students (papers in ED 47). The surviving files of these committees are in ED 71. University examining bodies helped in the administration of the scheme. ED 72 contains their annual reports on the selection of state scholars, statistics of successful and unsuccessful candidates and information about nominations and awards.

After the Education Act 1944, LEAs had to submit revised schemes for the provision of major awards, broadly bringing them into line with the value of state scholarships. By 1954 most LEAs had adopted the recommended levels of grant and selection standards. Files on these LEA schemes are in ED 153.

General files dealing with the provision of financial assistance for university education are in ED 54, including material on the Further Education and Training Scheme for ex-servicemen. This class also contains information about royal scholarships and studentships and other private sector prizes and awards.

11.5.2   National Council for Technological Awards

The National Council for Technological Awards (NCTA) was set up by the Minister of Education in 1955 in response to the recommendation by the National Advisory Council on Education for Industry that there should be a Council to create and administer a nationally recognized technological award for students of technical colleges. It was financed jointly by industry and central government and established under a trust deed as an independent self-governing body, with an executive committee, two boards of studies with a joint steering committee, a higher awards committee and subject panels. Files on the foundation of the Council and on its trust deed are in ED 46/758 and 759 respectively. Papers of the meetings of its constituent parts and its reports are in DB 1.

11.5.3   Council for National Academic Awards

One of the recommendations of the Robbins Committee was the establishment of a Council for National Academic Awards (CNAA). This body was set up by royal charter in 1964 (UGC 7/934-936) and its degrees replaced the former Diplomas in

Technology of the NCTA (*see 5.9.2*). By 1970 almost all University of London external degree courses had been superseded by ones recognized by the CNAA.

The CNAA was organized in a series of committees, whose minutes are available in DB 3. The annual reports of the Council are open without restriction in DB 2. Records of the National Council for Diplomas in Art and Design, which was absorbed by the CNAA in 1974, are in DB 4.

In 1962 the Minister of Education set up the National Committee for the Certificate in Office Studies. The committee had no formal terms of reference; its task was to draft detailed rules for the award of the certificate and to publish them with guidance notes. The course was introduced in 1963 and the committee remained in existence until 1975 approving syllabuses and monitoring progress. Papers relating to the early meetings of the committee are in ED 46/869-870, with later material in ED 200.

11.5.4   National Council for Educational Technology

The Brymor Jones report, *Audio visual aids in higher scientific education* (HMSO, 1965), led to the establishment two years later of the National Foundation for Educational Technology, a trust administered by the National Council for Educational Technology (NCET). The task of the NCET was to promote the application and development of inventions and techniques in the field of human learning and to promote research in educational technology. Information about the setting up of the NCET is in the Research and Planning General Files (ED 181); EA 1 contains its minutes and papers, with reports in EA 2..

11.5.5   B.Ed Degrees

One of the recommendations of the Robbins Committee on Higher Education in 1963 was for four year courses for teachers turning their teaching certificate into a B.Ed, to be awarded by the university with which the training college was associated. Initially, there was about a ten per cent take up of the B.Ed option. A House of Commons Select Committee, under F T Willey, which investigated teacher training in 1969-1970, criticized the lack of consultation and co-ordination. In 1972 the Council for National Academic Awards began validating B.Ed degrees and the following year the CNAA and the UGC jointly appointed a study group to draw up guidelines for a new B.Ed degree. In 1974 an integrated course of teacher training with the degree was recommended by the group.

11.6   Norwood Report

The connected subjects of schools examinations and curricula were examined by a committee of the SSEC, appointed in 1941 under Sir Cyril Norwood. Papers on the setting up of the committee and its work and report are in ED 138/16; ED 136/681; and ED 12/478-480.

Norwood reported directly to R A Butler in 1943 in the teeth of opposition from the SSEC . The committee's recommendations were finally accepted in 1946 by Ellen Wilkinson, Minister of Education, under circular 113/46 (ED 142/56) which altered the constitution of the SSEC and made the minister fully responsible for co-ordinating secondary school examinations. Some years after Norwood, the school certificate was replaced by the General Certificate of Education (GCE) in three levels: ordinary, advanced and scholarship. Norwood recommended that examinations should be subject rather than group based.

11.7   Beloe Report

GCE examinations were intended for the top twenty per cent of pupils but the demand for them was greater. As a result, the SSEC appointed the Beloe Committee in 1958 to look at examinations other than GCE (ED 147/303-313). Beloe recommended subject based public exams for those not suitable for GCE to be taken at sixteen plus, regionally organized and locally controlled. The SSEC was to draft papers for the Certificate of Secondary Education (CSE), introduced in 1965 as a less academic examination for secondary school children. Papers on its establishment and introduction are available as follows: ED147/655-682 general policy and individual subjects; ED 147/683-745 regional examining boards; ED 147/746-785 examinations; ED 147/869-878; EJ 1/12-15,19; EJ 2/8-9,13 Schools Council Committees on CSE.

11.8   Schools Council for Curriculum and Examinations

Traditionally the Ministry of Education had very little to do with the curriculum. In the debate in the House of Commons on the Crowther Report *15-18* (ED 146/29-44) David Eccles, the Minister for Education, referred to the 'secret garden of the curriculum', maintaining that Parliament should not just debate bricks and mortar and organization but also what was taught in schools.

As a result, the Curriculum Study Group was formed in 1962 within the ministry, consisting of HMIs, administrators and 'appropriate experts' (ED 147/786-811; EJ 1/2-3, 5, 65; EJ 2/2-3, 5). Derek Morrell, who headed the new body, suggested that it should combine with the Secondary Schools Examination Council to form a separate entity in which the curriculum led the examinations.

Sir Edward Boyle, Minister of Education, set up a working party under Sir John Lockwood, to examine this idea. The Lockwood Report recommended that an Independent Schools Council for Curriculum and Examinations be established, jointly financed by the LEAs and the Department of Education and Science (ED 147/812-816).

The Schools Council was set up in 1964 and assumed responsibility for most of the curriculum and examinations work formerly done by the SSEC and the Curriculum Study Group. Four years later, the constitution of the Schools Council was revised to strengthen the teachers' role and to abolish the distinction between the policy and executive divisions. In 1969 the Council became a registered charity.

In 1970 the Schools Council recommended a single examination at sixteen, to be co-ordinated by itself. After various trials, in 1976 the Council recommended to Shirley Williams, the Secretary of State for Education and Science, that the GCE and CSE should be replaced by a common system. The Secretary of State set up another study group of HMIs and DES representatives under Sir James Waddell. His group reported in 1978 and recommended new syllabuses by autumn 1983 and the first common examinations (General Certificate of Secondary Education) in 1985 (HC 1977/8 I, iix Cmnd 7281).

The report on standards *School Education in England: Problems and Initiatives*, known as the Yellow Book, ordered by James Callaghan, the Prime Minister, in 1976 criticised the performance of the Schools Council. This led to a second revision of the Council's constitution, reducing the dominance by teachers and giving financial control to the DES and LEA representatives. The constitution was revised a third time in 1984 to allow the Council to go into liquidation; the Secretary of State had announced two years earlier that the Council would be abolished and replaced by the Secondary Examinations Council and the School Curriculum Development Committee.

Documents relating to the work of the Schools Council are in ED 147/833-907,1344-1349. EJ 1 contains its agenda and minutes and the papers of its committees and working parties, with numbered papers of the Council in EJ 2; the files in both these classes are open immediately.

11.9   National Curriculum Council

The National Curriculum Council was created by the Education Reform Act 1988 to review the new national curriculum, advise the secretary of state upon it and to disseminate information about it. Its annual reports are in FW 1.

11.10   Case Study on Cookery

We can use the development of the study cookery in elementary schools, secondary schools and training colleges as an example of how to trace documents relating to one particular subject in the curriculum through the classes of education records. Cookery masquerades under several different guises: domestic economy, domestic subjects, practical instruction, handicraft, household and social science, housecraft, domestic science, home economics and most recently A/CDT (art/craft, design, technology).

11.10.1 Cookery in Elementary Schools to 1944

The Code for 1875 included domestic economy as a specific subject for the first time and made provision for the payment of a special grant - 4s for every girl in standard IV and above who passed the requisite examination satisfactorily. Further refinements in the regulations covering domestic economy were added in the Codes of 1878 and 1879. Those taking the subject rose from 844 in 1874 to 59,812 in 1882. These classes were in the theory of the subject only, without any practical work.

In 1877 school boards from such towns as Wolverhampton, Darlington, Sheffield and Birmingham petitioned the Education Department to make domestic economy analogous to chemistry and to provide practical instruction in cookery. The department was also asked to encourage female teachers to pass specific examinations to teach the subject (HC 1877 lxvii). A further petition along similar lines was received from female educationists in 1881, organized by Miss Florence Calder.

The Code for 1882 stated that special provision should be made for practical teaching. The 1885 Code not only laid down that at least twenty hours of the forty spent on domestic economy must be practical but also insisted that no more than twenty-four girls should attend the practice classes while seventy-two were allowed at demonstration lessons. These numbers were reduced to eighteen and fifty-four respectively in 1894.

The Codes of Regulations were published as Parliamentary papers and for the period up to 1900 copies are available in ED 17.

The London School Board had an enlightened attitude towards the teaching of cookery and introduced practice lessons in 1878 (ED 14/24). Practical cookery classes disrupted the use of classrooms and so special cookery centres were increasingly provided. Information about these separate premises in the capital can be found on the files of the London School Board (ED 14/1, 25, 37, 93, 104). After 1902 the LEAs set up similar centres (ED 11/2; *and see below*).

Miss Mary Harrison was appointed by the Education Department in 1890 as the first inspectress of cookery (T 1/8547C paper 348/91). She was succeeded in 1896 by Miss Hyacinthe Deane. When Miss Harrison took up her job, over 1,500 elementary schools were teaching cookery; six years later that number had risen to 2,729. Miss Deane oversaw the introduction in the Code for 1900 of a new combined course of Household Management, which included cookery, laundry work and housewifery. Her report on cookery and laundry work at the turn of the century is available in ED 24/68A. Other reports on the teaching of cookery in elementary schools during the 1890s are in ED 17/65-66,68-69.

The 1906 Code introduced new provisions for the teaching of domestic subjects in elementary schools: grant was awarded for each course, replacing the previous per capita system. Syllabuses had to be submitted to the Board of Education and additional women HMIs were appointed to inspect the practical instruction centres where these subjects were sometimes taught.

LEA files on these centres are in ED 96. Surviving material includes: lists of premises proposed for the recognition of courses; establishment of centres; arrangements for instruction; HMI general reports; annual returns of premises and changes in them. The complementary series of files on particular centres are in ED 70 and relate to the provision of courses (eg in domestic economy and cookery), acquisition of land and buildings, more HMI reports, and applications for course approval.

11.10.1.1 Special Reports on the Teaching of Cookery 1897, 1905, 1907 and 1912

Margaret Pillow, an examiner for the National Training School of Cookery (*see below*) wrote a report on *Domestic Economy Teaching in England* in 1897 in which she described the progress since 1870. Alice Ravenhill, an inspector of hygiene and domestic economy in Yorkshire, visited the USA in 1901 and produced a lengthy and detailed report on *The Teaching of Domestic Science in the USA*. Both these studies were published in the series of 'Sadler Special Reports' on the curriculum in 1897 and 1905 respectively.

In a memo of 1904 about the appointment of the first chief woman inspector, Robert Morant, permanent secretary to the Board of Education, expressed the following opinion:

> such cookery as is taught in the Public Elementary School should be supervised by a woman, thoroughly versed, if you will, in the practical art of cookery; but that such a woman inspector should be constantly supervised by a woman who has not carried Cookery Investigation to such a high pitch, and who has preserved a firm realisation of the due place which cookery should fill in the school life of the children in question
>
> ED 23/152B

The formation of the Women Inspectorate, which included several teachers of domestic subjects, provided the opportunity for a report into the teaching of cookery in public elementary schools by the chief woman inspector in 1905-1906. The investigation was carried out by the female HMI who had experience of teaching domestic subjects. They reported on the teaching staff, the length of lessons (including the gap between demonstration lessons and practice classes), registers, note books and record books, the sale of food and the character and suitability of dishes prepared.

The report recommended: that the gap in the timetable between demonstration and practice classes should be reduced; that the arrangement to sell the food prepared in these classes led to a narrow approach with unsuitable recipes; and that more cheap, simple, wholesome cooking should be taught. It advised that the classes must be educational and that deficient note books could be improved by inspection. Teachers were said to welcome the advice of HMIs.

This was followed by a second report published five years later. It showed that improvements had been made: more practical instruction was being provided; recipes were more appropriate to the background of the pupils; more regular inspections had been carried out; the numbers of cookery centres had risen from 1,771 in 1907 to 2,902 in 1911 and the number of classes had increased from 702 to 806, although they still did not reach all the appropriate elementary school girls. It pointed to the assistance provided by the forty-four countywide organizers of domestic subjects and to the difficulties experienced in rural areas. Boys were asking for cookery instruction.

These reports, entitled *Special Report on the Teaching of Cookery to Public Elementary School Children in England Wales* and *General Report on the Teaching of Domestic Subjects to Public Elementary School Children in England and Wales,* were published by the Board of Education in 1907 and 1912 respectively. Copies are available in ED 11/169 and held at the Department for Education and Employment Information Bureau (*see under Useful Addresses*). Background material to the 1907 report is in ED 11/60.

Reports by HMI Miss Rowlands on the teaching of domestic subjects in Welsh elementary schools between 1912 and 1923 are in ED 92/10 and 12.

11.10.1.2 Between the wars

Under section 2 of the Education Act 1918 (re-enacted as section 20 of the Education Act 1921) LEAs were given the duty of providing for practical instruction in elementary schools. The Hadow Report, *Education and the Adolescent*, published in 1926, established the principle that, as far as possible, practical instruction should be the responsibility of senior schools. Information about the teaching of domestic subjects in elementary and higher elementary schools will be found in ED 11/169-170 and 278. These files also contain information about an investigation into allegations that girls were reluctant to enter domestic service. ED 11/278 provides details about the teaching of domestic subjects in Sussex in the mid 1930s.

A departmental committee was set up in 1937 to look at the teaching of cookery. Papers on appointments to serve on the committee are in ED 136/647 and its working papers are in ED 11/249 and ED 136/690.

11.10.2 Cookery in Secondary Schools to 1944

Margaret Pillow's report of 1897 showed that the teaching of domestic economy in secondary schools was very uneven. It was regarded as an inferior subject in girls independent schools and provided 'for girls not taking otherwise too many subjects'. The Regulations for Secondary Schools issued in 1909 stated that:

> Provision should be made in the case of girls for instruction of a practical character in the elements of housewifery. For girls of 15 years of age an approved course in Domestic Subjects may be taken instead of Science.

Secondary schools were unsure how to respond and, although housecraft in the curriculum for girls' schools had been referred to the Consultative Committee in 1909, they asked for some immediate guidance.

This was provided by the Interim Memorandum (ED 12/43) which saw housecraft as:

> an integral part of the curriculum of secondary schools for girls, and as such requiring definition, development, and encouragement

The memorandum gave some examples of schemes of work in various types of secondary school; attempting a correlation between science and housecraft, it coined the term 'domestic science'. In practice, schools were left fairly free to resolve the curriculum problems in their own way and given freedom to experiment; the Board would accept the minimum interpretation of the regulations.

Meanwhile an Inspectorate Committee on Housecraft was set up in May 1910 under the chairmanship of Dr R P Scott. His committee reported in December 1910. A copy of its report is in ED 12/43 and other related papers are in ED 12/41 and 42; ED 24/386; ED 23/90 and ED 93/2. The Inspectorate gathered evidence for the broader Consultative Committee report (ED 22/37; ED 24/213,1225), which was published in 1913 (HC 1913 xx Cd 6849).

ED 12/41 contains information from 1907 to 1911 on the contemporary debate: copies of a series of articles by Alice Ravenhill for *Education* in 1908; reports from selected GPDST schools with typical syllabuses; and requests from LEAs to extend the examination syllabus to cover home economics. Housecraft was accepted as a subject for school certificate only in 1931.

11.10.3 After 1944

The papers of the panel for Housecraft, later Home Economics, are in ED 158/129-143 and cover the period 1943 to 1972. They include reports of working parties on the subject, HMI surveys of home economics and various discussion papers.

ED 147/263-265 are the files of the Secondary Schools Examination Council subject panel on housecraft and cover the years 1951-1964. Papers on preparations for the CSE examination in the subject 1961-1962 are in ED 147/662.

For twenty years from 1964 to 1984 the curriculum came under the influence of the Schools Council (EJ 1 and EJ 2). Minutes of the Home Economics Committee and its sub committees are in EJ 1/121-124, with the papers which those committees produced or considered in EJ 2.

11.10.4 Training Schools

At the third International Exhibition in 1873, J C Buckmaster, organizing master of the Science and Art Department, lectured on cookery. This stimulated an interest in cookery which was quickly followed up by the founding of a National Training School of Cookery. Similar schools were established in Liverpool, Leeds, Manchester and Leicester. These were all private ventures. Exceptionally, the papers of the National Training School are available in ED 164 and its minute books can be used to trace the development of the school during the nineteenth century (ED 164/1-26).

These training schools taught by demonstration lessons and gradually introduced practice classes. They taught 'household cookery' suited to their middle class clientele but were also involved in evening classes at continuation schools. More training schools were set up between 1890 and 1894 with the increasing interest in technical education coupled with the availability of 'whisky money' (*see 5.2.4*). These schools flourished at Bath, Battersea, Cardiff, Gloucester, Newcastle, and Preston. The National Society started its own school in Hampstead in 1893, later known as Berridge House.

The Education Department became increasingly involved with these training schools. In 1877 it issued a circular encouraging the use of teachers from the National Training School (ED 142/36). A two-tier diploma system developed, with the better training schools requiring six months work for the qualification and others issuing local diplomas involving much less work and much less competence. A departmental committee was appointed to recommend a minimum standard of training. This led to the circular of 1893 defining conditions under which diplomas would be recognized (ED 142/37).

In 1896 the Education Department recognized twenty-seven training schools. To gain recognition, the schools had to be open to inspection by the department and follow an approved timetable and scheme of work for training teachers of cookery. In 1899 the department set up its own examination for a cookery diploma. The inspectress of cookery, Hyacinthe Deane, and two assistants were to administer this three times a year in each training school as well as carrying out their routine inspections. These examinations were abandoned in 1907. ED 24/58A contains copies of Miss Deane's reports on cookery teaching for 1899 and 1900 and cookery examination papers of the same date.

The Regulations for Technical Schools of 1905 introduced the first grants for teachers of domestic subjects. Gradually a full two year course in cookery, laundry work and housewifery replaced diplomas in single subjects. By 1910 all training schools outside London, except Liverpool and Preston, were under LEA control; this was made possible by the grant system. Finally, in 1918 training schools for domestic subjects attained the same status as other training colleges when uniform grants were introduced. Details of these are available in circulars 1036 and 1041 of that year (ED 142/46). The demand from secondary schools for more specialized teachers led the training colleges to submit schemes for more advanced work and syllabuses; some became eligible for grants for third year approved courses.

ED 115/91 is a memorandum on ten domestic science training colleges visited in 1931 (Berridge House, Hampstead; Westminster School of Cookery; Battersea Polytechnic; Newcastle upon Tyne; Leeds; Liverpool; Manchester; Bath; Gloucester; Leicester). Recommendations include improving their libraries in the housecraft section.

Details of files on individual training colleges will be found in the appendix to this chapter.

11.10.5 Teachers of Domestic Subjects

Teachers of domestic subjects only gradually acquired equivalent status to others in the profession. In 1913 the Royal Society of Teachers first admitted domestic science teachers. They became eligible for superannuation and similar salary scales during the Burnham negotiations in 1919. ED 24/1789 contains papers relating to teachers of domestic subjects between 1912 and 1921. The first representative for domestic subjects on the Central Advisory Committee for the Certification of Teachers was appointed in 1930. By the end of the Second World War, however, during the emergency recruitment of teachers, special courses were laid on for teachers of domestic subjects (ED 143/23).

11.10.6 Higher Education

King's College started a three year course in home and social science in 1908 just as the college was incorporated into the University of London. The course was attached to the Women's Department of King's College, under philosophy and science. This department became King's College for Women in 1910. A recommendation of the Haldane Commission (*see 7.2.5*) that the Home and Social Science Department become independent led to new buildings on Campden Hill, which opened in 1916.

This was an attempt to intellectualize the subject and to bring scientific knowledge to bear on household matters. Its scope was extended to include economics, the effects of industrialization and poverty. The term 'household' replaced 'home' in 1916 and the first examination was held two years later. In 1920 the University of London recognized a three year B.Sc course in Household and Social Science, with a fourth year of professional training to qualify for a teaching diploma.

In 1927 Bristol University and Gloucester Training College began a joint four year course leading to a B.Sc (Dom Sc) degree. Circular 1372 of 1925 (ED 142/50) announced that the Board of Education would discontinue examining students in training colleges of domestic subjects from 1929 when they would be associated with universities like other training college students. This was one of the recommendations of the Departmental Committee for the Training of Teachers for the formation of Joint Examination Boards (*see 9.8 above*). Three London colleges linked up with King's College, London; Calder College and Manchester College joined Manchester University; Bath, Gloucester and Leicester Colleges joined Bristol University; Northern Counties College and Newcastle upon Tyne joined Durham University; and South Wales and Monmouth College joined the University of Wales.

GUITE TO FILES ON PARTICULAR COLLEGES OF DOMESTIC SUBJECTS			
College	**Files**	**Endowment**	**Inspectorate Reports**
National Training College Westminster estab 1873	ED 164/1-26 (1873-1962) ED 78/47, 133, 407-408 (1932-1955)	ED 40/67-68	ED 115/57-58
Leeds estab 1874	ED 78/70 (1932-1933) ED 78/559 (1946-1955)		ED 115/86 (1913)
Leicester estab 1874	ED 78/31, 113,349-352 (vd 1932-1955)		ED 115/37-38 (vd 1913-1930) ED 115/133 (1946-1947)
Manchester estab 1874 and 1880	ED 78/27 (1925-1935) ED 78/111 (1936-1944) ED 78/323-324 (1947-1955)		ED 115/33 (1920) ED 115/130 (1947)

Liverpool: F L Calder estab by 1877	ED 78/25 (1928-1935) ED 78/107 (1945) ED 78/309 (1946-1947)		ED 115/29-31 (vd 1913-1931) ED 115/125 (1953)
Sheffield: Totley Hall estab 1889	ED 78/571-574 (1948-1955)		ED 115/90 (1913)
Gloucestershire estab 1890	ED 78/18 (1932-1935) ED 78/99 (1937 -1940) ED 78/270-271 (1948-1955)		ED 115/20-22 (vd 1913-1935) ED 115/115 (1947-1948)
S Wales and Monmouthshire estab 1891	ED 78/599 (1946-1955)		ED 115/96-98 (vd 1921-1934) ED 115/169 (1946-1955)
Northern Counties: Newcastle upon Tyne estab 1893	ED 78/143 (1937-1942) ED 78/434-436 (1946-1955)		ED 115/69-70 (1912,1924) ED 115/144 (1953)
National Society: Hampstead Berridge House estab 1893	ED 78/40 (1932 -1934) ED 78/125 (1937-1945) ED 78/379 (1946-1948)		ED 115/49-50 (vd 1913-1921) ED 115/139 (1948-1949)
Bath estab 1894	ED 78/57 (1932 -1935) ED 78/147 (1940-1944) ED 78/458-462 (1945-1955)		ED 115/74-75 (1913,1925) ED 115/147 (1951)
Preston estab 1894			ED 115/34 (1913)

King's College estab 1908			ED 115/41B (1931-1933)
Battersea	ED 78/35 (1932 -1935) ED 78/117 (1937-1945) ED 78/36336-4 (1946-1955)		ED 115/41-43 (vd 1912-1947) ED 115/135 (1954)
Ilkley	ED 78/552-554 (1949-1955)		
Radbrook	ED 78/439-442 (1946-1954)		
Seaford	ED 78/488-489 (1948-1955)		

11.11   List of classes

Council for National Academic Awards

1.   National Council for Technological Awards 1945-1965 (DB 1)
-        reports and papers of council and its governing body; minutes of committees, boards and panels

2.   Annual Reports 1964-1991 (DB 2)

3.   Minutes 1964-1985 (DB 3)

4.   National Council for Diplomas in Art and Design 1961-1974 (DB 4)
-        minutes of council and its specialist panels

National Council for Educational Technology

1.   Minutes and Papers 1967-1988 (EA 1)

2.   Reports 1967-1994 (EA 2)
-        special and annual reports

12   BUILDINGS

12.1   Elementary Schools

12.1.1   Voluntary Schools pre-1870

Information about sites for voluntary schools can be found among the enrolled deeds on the Close Rolls (C 54); four volumes of similar deeds, mostly relating to elementary schools, and dating from 1903 to 1920 are in ED 191 (*see also 3.2 above*). Other related records which give details about premises are the building grant applications (ED 103) and the preliminary statements (ED 7). Chapter 3.3 contains a description of the system of building grants for voluntary schools administered by the PCCE and the Treasury and the records which relate to it. For a detailed account of the Trust Deeds and building grant application relating to Lower Bebington voluntary school in Cheshire see the case study at 3.14. The PCCE issued detailed specifications for the work including precise instructions to the various craftsmen (eg mason, slater, bricklayer, plasterer, smith, etc) and plans of possible buildings. Copies are available in ED 17/3 and 4.

Most plans associated with the individual applications are preserved in local record offices but a small selection of proposed plans and drawings for elementary schools survives in ED 228 for the period 1843-1872. ED 228/82 includes a specification of works and material used in the erection of new schools and a teacher's residence and ED 228/99 contains a plan and information about William Porritt's air-warming underground stoves. Sometimes the Preliminary Statements (ED 7) are accompanied by plans of various sorts. ED 7/138, for example, contains several plans; one of Ruswarp National School near Whitby, is a full page ground plan in colour on a scale of 8' to 1".

HMI E M Sneyd-Kinnersley commented on the pre-1870 voluntary schools built by the National Society:

> they build generously, 'if not according to knowledge', strange schools in the University-Gothic style; externally picturesque; internally ill-lighted, ill-ventilated, ill-warmed, but no worse than you would find in the great public schools.

12.1.2   Board Schools 1870-1902

The Parish Files (ED 2) contain the returns made by parishes to the school accommodation census provided for under the Forster Act 1870, as well as other general correspondence and papers about accommodation and the provision of new schools. Similar returns for London parishes are in ED 3, for parishes with only one

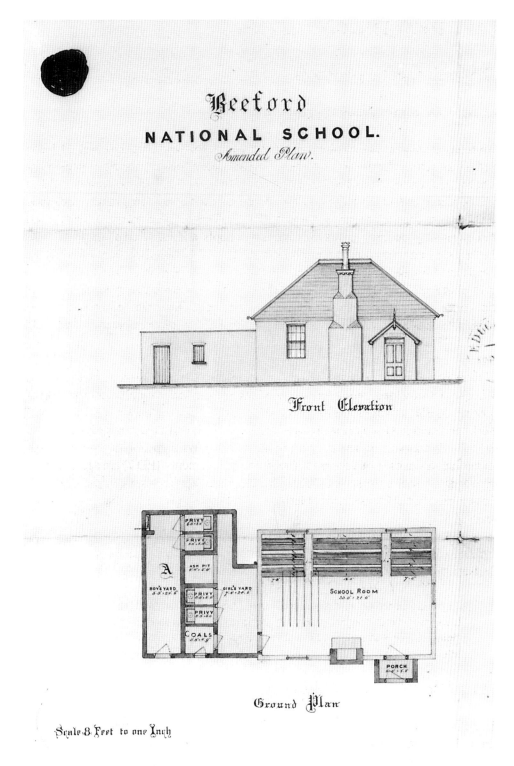

Figure 17
Plan of Beeford National School, 1870 (ED 228/67)

Figure 18
Scene in a classroom at Leys School, Cambridge, 1930s (INF 9/432)

school in ED 21 and for municipal boroughs in ED 16. See 3.5 for further details about these records and their interrelation.

Provision was made under the 1870 Act for elementary schools in the London area to be transferred to the London School Board. This process included the completion of a form containing a description of the buildings; 106 files containing these details are in ED 4. Other material relating to the 'supply', ie accommodation, of schools administered by the London School Board is in ED 14 (especially ED 14/1-16, 27-29, 45, 49).

MH 27/130-142 are further files of correspondence between the London School Board and the Education Department; most of the papers relate to auditing the LSB accounts. MH 27/130 in the section for 1875 contains a number of completed 'supply form no 7' for individual schools which give the following building details:

> size of rooms
> total square footage
> teacher's residence
> costs of the site, buildings, etc
> architect's commission
> other building expenses, eg fittings

The volume also includes a list payments to suppliers of furniture and fittings in 1873 but there is no indication of what the individual items were.

In order to provide buildings it was sometimes necessary for school boards to purchase land compulsorily. Procedures were laid down for this under the 1870 Act and the papers containing the petitions for compulsory purchase by individual school boards are in ED 5. Sometimes elementary school buildings or a fund for their upkeep had been provided as part of an endowment; material on such endowments is in ED 49.

For capital expenditure, ie building new schools, boards could borrow from the Public Works Loans Commissioners (PWLC), against the security of the rates. The Department scrutinized all such applications to fill in the gaps very carefully and if a board built a school the Department considered superfluous it could refuse grant. The Department vetted all applications for loans from the PWLC. Favourable rates of interest were allowed to school boards after the 1870 Act but after 1879 the PWLC began to vary interest rates.

In 1888 the building requirements were rewritten: all schools had to provide 10 sq ft per child (previously 8 and originally 6). Additional grants were made available only for very poor rural areas. By 1890 the building regulations referred explicitly to healthy, adequately ventilated and well lit buildings. These regulations were printed as part of the Code and copies are in ED 17.

12.1.3   Voluntary Schools post-1870

Building grants were abolished in 1870 but voluntary schools were given six months grace in which to submit applications. These grants were all cleared by 1882. Between 1876 and 1886 there were sixty-one applications for annual grant from new voluntary schools in school board districts. Eighteen school boards waived their right to fill the gap but forty-three boards refused to recognize voluntary schools in their districts, forcing the Education Department to refuse them grant. Sometimes voluntary schools were taken over by school boards. Evidence of this should be found in the institution files in ED 21 or the parish files (ED 2).

12.1.4   Poor Law Schools

Under the new poor law pauper children could be educated in schools attached to the workhouse. After 1846 they might be sent to district or 'barrack' schools, large institutions in rural areas which poor law unions banded together to build. From 1861, guardians could send workhouse children to the local elementary school and the 1870 Act extended this option. By the end of the century district schools were being replaced by 'cottage homes', housing about fifteen children and many pupils were educated in local elementary schools; sometimes they were boarded out to do so.

Information about poor law school buildings attached to workhouses will be found in MH 12, under the appropriate union. MH 27 contains details about the construction and upkeep of thirteen of the fourteen district schools (Central London, South Metropolitan, North Surrey, Farnham and Hartley Wintney, S E Shropshire, Reading and Wokingham, Kensington, Lincoln and Nottinghamshire, West London, Forest Gate, Walsall West Bromwich, Kensington and Chelsea, Brentwood). After 1904 responsibility for the remaining poor law schools was transferred to the education authorities and surviving files on these schools are in ED 132.

12.1.5   Building Survey 1893

The annual inspection of an elementary school automatically included a survey of the adequacy of the buildings and equipment. It had long been known that conditions in older schools were not up to standard and in circular 321 of 1893 inspectors were asked to report on the facilities and buildings of every school they visited. A copy of the circular and the accompanying form is in ED 24/56B. Information about this survey may be found on the school files (ED 21) or the parish files (ED 2). The majority of schools with deficient buildings were voluntary ones.

Building regulations were amplified and tightened up in subsequent codes. Between April 1894 and October 1895, 157 schools were warned that grants would be withheld unless defects were remedied within three years. Payment to twenty-one schools was suspended for three months while repairs were made. Quarterly returns of schools warned were printed for Parliament.

12.1.6 Elementary Schools after 1902

Information about elementary school buildings after they became the responsibility of the LEAs continues to be on the Institution Files in ED 21 and the Supply Files in ED 16. ED 70 and ED 96 contain information about practical instruction centre buildings. Details of nursery school provision after 1918 will be found in ED 66, together with the results of the LEA survey of nursery schools carried out in 1936 and the supply of nursery schools for the children of women war workers. Related files are in ED 69 and ED 102.

Papers on accommodation in London schools between 1900 and 1920 are in ED 14/59-87, arranged by borough. Policy files on school premises and equipment during this period are in ED 24 Code 44. Correspondence with LEAs between 1904 and 1910 about the 9 and 10 square feet policy are in ED 24/354-365. (*See also 12.6.*)

12.1.7 Black List Schools

In 1908 the Board of Education, with the help of the Inspectorate, drew up a Black List of schools which needed improvement to their buildings. The Inspectorate memoranda include some memos on the process (ED 22/8, 1908 no 26; ED 22/10, 1910 nos 47-49; and for Welsh schools ED 22/82, 1908 nos 5 and 11). A black-listed school could fall into one the four categories described by R Walrond in a letter dated 13 May 1913 (ED 14/57). Schedule I included schools which had been notified that official recognition of the existing premises would cease on 30 April 1915; schedule II schools were described as premises whose defects did not admit remedy and any considerable expenditure on the premises would be thrown away; schedule III covered those schools which needed substantial improvements if their Board of Education recognition was to continue; and premises that fell into schedule IV had defects which were considered less grave but still prejudicial to the efficient conduct of the school. The aim of the Black List was to force the LEAs to make the repairs.

EXAMPLE:

ED 21/15195

Flax Bourton elementary school in Somerset was served with a schedule iv notice in March 1911 stating that it was unsatisfactory in heating and lavatory accommodation.

ED 14/51-52 contain information about defective schools in London and ED 14/57 is a black list of voluntary schools in London. The supply files for individual London boroughs (ED 14/59-87) include reports on Black List schools. A departmental committee was set up in 1910 to examine the cost of school buildings; its papers are available in ED 10/4-9.

Improvements were made up to the First World War. The Black List scheme was revived in 1924 by memorandum E 271 to the HMI. This time the Black List was divided into three categories A, B and C, and LEAs were informed and asked to arrange remedial action. ED 99 contains the reports by HMIs, minutes and memoranda on the compilation of the Black Lists and correspondence about the improvements made and progress achieved. The files are arranged by counties and county boroughs. ED 24 Code 44 contains further policy files on the Black Lists; instances of defective Welsh schools are referred to in ED 92/13 and 24.

Despite the action on Black List schools, and the seminal reports from the Consultative Committee on the structure of primary education, little new building was done in the inter-war years. Economy was the watch word, particularly for elementary schools. The Baines Committee of 1925 sought to cut classroom areas per pupil from 10-12 square feet to 9-10 and to remove all frills. The Departmental Committee on the Cost of School Buildings, chaired by Sir Frank Baines, was asked to look at not only the use of new materials and methods of construction but also the reduction of cost. A copy of the report of the committee is in ED 24/1616.

12.2 Technical and Further Education

12.2.1 Science and Art Department

The Science and Art Department introduced building grants for art schools in 1856 and extended them to science schools in 1868. These grants were conditional and for a maximum of £500. They ceased in 1896 but outstanding claims were dealt with until 1904. Grants were also made towards fittings, apparatus and diagrams until 1890 when 'whisky money' became available (*see 5.2.4 above*). ED 29 contains the files on these grants. The papers include: minutes, memoranda and correspondence on the sale of premises; specifications of work, plans and designs; grant details and information about withdrawn or refused applications; and some copy deeds and conveyances. Further correspondence and papers relating to art and science school buildings are in WORK 17, with plans in WORK 33.

12.2.2 Further Education after 1900

The institution files listed at the end of chapter 5 contain information about premises. ED 46, the Further Education General Files cover the problems of supplying the accommodation. A survey of technical building and art accommodation in regional areas was carried out by HMIs in 1935 (ED 46/105-114). A similar investigation took place between 1936 and 1943 into buildings for small technical schools (ED 46/253) A general review of further education building was carried out between 1948 and 1955; it included suggested priorities and a national approach to long term building (ED 46/697-698).

12.3 Training Colleges and Pupil-Teacher Centres

Building grants for normal schools (training colleges) were first introduced in 1835 (*see above 9.2*). ED 103/140 contains building grant applications for training colleges up to 1870; the volume is indexed. The following files survive among the Treasury Board Papers on training college building grants for the period up to 1851:

1841	T 1/4595/13542
1844	5010/24230
1847	5328/29027
1848	5388/18601
	5420/25908
1849	5457/7742
	5499/9779
1850	T 1/5542/326
	5552/6110
	5555/7899
	5583A/18490
1851	T 1/5634B/1599
	5644B/6740
	5646A/7440
	5654A/10700
	5654A/10909
	5661A/14025
	5661A/14026
	5683B/21052

The PCCE bought an estate in Middlesex, called Kneller Hall, in 1847 to develop as a normal school (*see above 9.2*). Various building work was done there during the decade of ownership. Information about this also survives among the Treasury papers:

1847	T 1/5313/27240	1853	T 1/5827B/22546
1848	5422/26206	1854	5907B/26566
1859	5526/27432	1855	5907A/19814
1850	5621/25274	1856	6037A/19996
1851	5689A/22429	1857	6070A/11594

Endowment files relating to teacher training colleges are in ED 40. The earlier papers were transferred from the Charity Commission under the Board of Education Act 1899. Information about the acquisition, enlargement and improvement of pupil-teacher centres (and school board offices where the two functions were carried out in combined premises) is in ED 57 (*see also 9.3 above*).

In order to meet the shortfall of training college buildings, the Regulations for 1906 offered seventy-five per cent building grants to LEAs for capital expenditure on acquisition, erection, enlargement or improvement of college buildings. Avery Hill was the first college to benefit from this grant (ED 87/10). In 1909 it was extended to universities and university colleges. The scheme lasted until 1922 for projects started pre-war but no new grants were accepted. Applications for this grant-aid are in ED 87 together with ancillary supporting documents.

Related later files are in ED 86, ED 78 and ED 159. The expansion of buildings in the late 1950s and 1960s for teacher training colleges and Institutes of Education attached to the University of Wales is covered in ED 217 and includes plans and photographs.

12.4   Secondary Schools to 1944

The main series of Institution Files on secondary schools (ED 35) contains some information about the premises.

EXAMPLES:

ED 35/1476   Wyggeston Boys Grammar School, Leicester

Includes papers on proposed new buildings in 1914 with conditions for competitive tenderers and a plan of the new site. Later in the file there are more discussions of new buildings as well as an architect's estimate of the cost (£37,693). The file ends with further correspondence about the availability of the Old Asylum site, then a military hospital, as an extension, in association with a new university college for Leicester.

ED 35/2443   Sutton High School (GPDST) Sutton, Surrey

File includes correspondence about the purchase of adjoining land, with a surveyor's report on the proposed purchase. There is also a specification for additional classrooms and a large plan drawn up in 1918, as well as blue prints for the extra accommodation.

The Endowment Files (ED 27) also include details about the acquisition or sale of land for endowed secondary schools and should be seen in conjunction with the Estate Management Files (ED 43). Policy files on secondary schools and equipment are in ED 12 Code 10/3 and include papers on the revision of building rules: 1912-1921 (ED 12/140-141), 1924-1930 (ED 12/373); and Educational Pamphlet No 86 on

Secondary School Buildings 1930-1931 (ED 12/375). Other related policy papers are in ED 24 Code 44 and ED 136/14-16.

For a detailed account of information on premises relating to Kendrick Girls' School see case study at 4.10 above.

12.5   Post-war building

Information about payments to non-provided schools by the War Damage Commission will be found in ED 136/562.

An extract from the minutes of the Inspectorate central panel in April 1948 gives an indication of the state of school buildings after the war:

> of the 167 schools in this district there remain two with reactivated earth closets, 41 with wooden seats over pails, 84 with wooden seats over vaults or ditches which are emptied half-yearly in a very few cases but which usually remain untouched for at least a year and sometimes for four or five years . . .
>
> ED 176/2

The condition of existing schools in addition to the post-war education plans which had far-reaching implications for buildings (eg separate primary and secondary schools, replacement of Black List and bombed schools, raising school leaving age, demand for more technical education and teacher training) made forecasting the cost of a building programme problematic. Some estimates, prepared by Sir Robert Wood, deputy secretary to the Board of Education will be found in ED 10/285 and ED 136/336.

Sir Robert also chaired two committees on school planning (ED 136/338, 680). The first one was formed in January 1942 and drew up its report within two months. Its recommendations included: standardization of construction on a grid system; one form one classroom; and a separate dining room. Drawings were ready by May and then the committee consulted interested parties. The Ministry of Works pressed for wider consultation, and a second committee was formed with representatives from the LEAs, teachers, architects and the building industry. Its report, published in summer 1944, came to broadly the same conclusion but was more conciliatory in tone. The papers of both these committees are in ED 136/680. Before the Ministry could build a 'demonstration school', private building firms had adopted the standardization approach (ED 10/285; ED 150/3-4). Related papers on post-war reconstruction and the school building programme are in ED 136/334 and 336.

12.5.1   HORSA and SFORSA

Raising the school leaving age from fourteen to fifteen was a central plank in post-war planning but it required an additional 400,000 school places. In May 1945 the

Ministry announced plans for a Hutting Operation for Raising the School-Leaving Age (HORSA) (circular 48 ED 142/55). The operation was to be 'outside the scope of the development plans' being drawn up by LEAs (ED 152). The Royal Institute of British Architects (RIBA) objected to the designs but the Ministry defended its initiative (ED 136/680 and ED 150/4). HORSA was combined with the School Furniture Operation for Raising the School-Leaving Age (SFORSA). The Ministry's annual report for 1949 showed that between April 1945 and June 1949, 146,445 primary and secondary places were provided in hutted accommodation.

12.5.2   Architects and Building Branch

The A and B Branch, as it was known, was set up in 1949 in order to bring together work previously carried out in three separate branches (schools, further education and teacher training) and to co-ordinate all aspects of educational building. The Education Act 1944 laid down uniform building regulations for educational establishments; previously each LEA building scheme had been considered on its merits. A system of annual building programmes was announced in 1947 for introduction in 1949 and eleven regional priority officers were appointed to liaise with other government departments at the regional level and to resolve the problems created by shortages of labour and materials (these posts were abolished in 1955 because they were no longer necessary). These new arrangements are outlined in the following Establishment Files: A and B Branch ED 23/899; territorial team organization ED 23/902; regional priority officers ED 23/919, 936.

In 1952 the A and B branch was the subject of an internal inquiry. The Sub-committee of the Cabinet Building Committee asked for an enquiry into the building policy and practice of the Ministry of Education, hoping to obtain sufficient evidence to criticize educational building and the allocation of capital and materials. Contrary to popular expectations, however, the inquiry, led by W H Pilkington, vindicated the work of the A and B branch in all aspects. A copy of this report can be seen at the Department for Education and Employment Information Bureau *(see useful addresses)*.

ED 150 contains the main registered files of the A and B Branch, which includes the papers of the working party responsible for the new standardized building regulations. These files also cover the work of the Development Group on control of the building programmes, analysis of the costs and administration of the building regulations. A new registered file series was introduced in the A and B Branch in 1965 and those papers are in ED 203. Technical publications issued by the branch on the design and building of educational premises are in ED 173. The Chief Architects of Consortia Committee (CAOC) was formed by the DES in 1964 to act as a forum for the exchange of information and for discussion of technical building policy. ED 199 contains minutes and papers of CAOC between 1967 and 1971.

LEA files on major building projects are in ED 154 (schools on new housing estates, accommodation shortages in existing schools and additional places required by raising

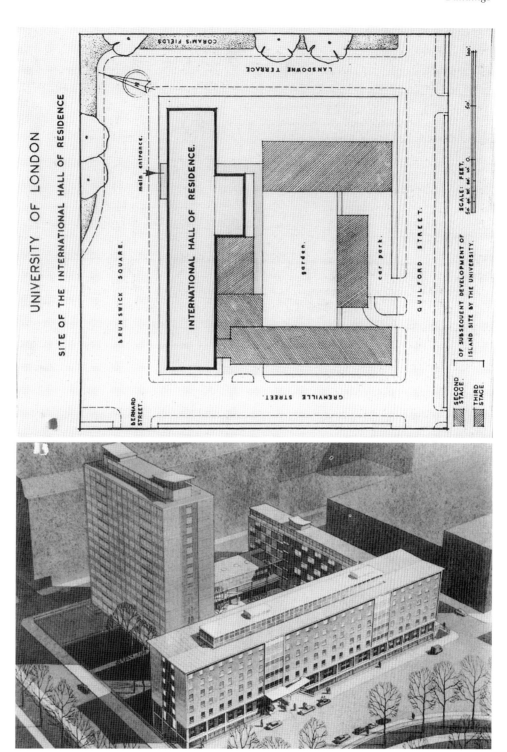

Figure 19
Plan and elevation of the proposed International Hall of Residence, University of London, 1950s (UGC 7/569)

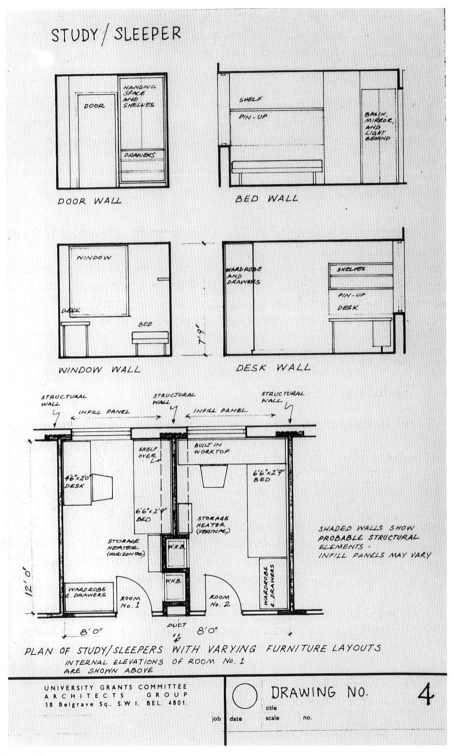

Figure 20
Plans for a 'study/sleeper' in a hall of residence, 1963 (UGC 7/574)

the school leaving age in 1947). Most of these projects arose from the development plans submitted by LEAs under the 1944 Act (ED 152). Papers on the major building programme resulting from the circular on comprehensive education (10/65) are in ED 147/822-824.

Files on other building programmes are arranged as follows: Further Education in ED 40/1022-1031 and ED 160; national colleges in ED 165; major direct grant college premises in ED 166; major art colleges in ED 167; regional and local colleges in ED 168.

12.6 Universities

The registered files of the University Grants Committee include papers on the post-war acquisition of sites and buildings for new universities (UGC 7/372-540, 950-959). The purchase of Whiteknights Park, by the future Reading University, for example, contains plans and photographs (UGC 7/959) and the papers on the building of Imperial College of Science and Technology also include plans (UGC 7/880-894). Other material on the university building works programme is in UGC 7/987-1056.

12.7 List of Classes

12.7.1 Institution Files

12.7.1.1 Elementary Education

1. Chancery Close Rolls 1204-1903 (C 54)
   - from 1725 private conveyances of land in trust for schools enrolled on dorse (back)

2. Legal Branch: Enrolled Deeds 1903-1920 (ED 191)
   - four volumes of deeds enrolled under Mortmain and Charitable Trusts Acts 1888-1892 and Technical and Industrial Institutions Act 1892; mostly for public elementary schools

3. Building Grant Applications 1833-1881 (ED 103)
   - application for grants towards cost of erecting public elementary schools

4. Public Elementary Schools: Preliminary Statements 1846-1924 (ED 7)
   - tenure and foundation; accounts; accommodation; staffing

5. Committee of the Privy Council on Education, Minutes and Reports 1839-1899 (ED 17)
   - instructions and plans for buildings

6.   Sealed Plans and Drawings 1843-1872 (ED 228)
       -     some of the coloured plans and elevations of school buildings
             accompanying building grant applications

7.   Elementary Education: Parish Files 1872-1904 (ED 2)
       -     educational census returns and reports from schools outside London
             and boroughs c1871; accommodation; school boards; new schools;
             loan sanctions

8.   Elementary Education: London Educational Returns 1871 (ED 3)
       -     educational census returns for London; types of schools; classrooms;
             school income; inspectors reports

9.   Ministry of Education and predecessors: Public Elementary School Files
       1857- 1946 (ED 21)
       -     statistics and information about school premises, accommodation,
             inspection and organization

10.   Elementary Education: Local Education Authority Supply Files 1870-1945
       (ED 16)
       -     including educational returns for boroughs and other urban areas
             c.1871; accommodation

11.   Public Elementary Schools: Preliminary Statements 1846-1924 (ED 7)
       -     tenure and foundation; accounts; accommodation; staffing

12.   Elementary Education, Compulsory Purchase Files 1873-1922 (ED 5)
       -     includes petitions, schedules, plans of land, statutory declarations and
             similar documents, correspondence with inspectors and reports from
             them on the sites concerned

13.   Treasury Board Papers 1557-1920 (T 1)
       -     contain similar applications and correspondence with PC Committee
             on Education on school building grants 1833-1902

12.7.1.2 Practical Instruction Centres and other Centres

1.   Practical Instruction Centre Files 1906-1957 (ED 70)
       -     includes documentation on the acquisition of land and buildings

16.   Major Arts Establishments 1931-1974 (ED 167)
       -     records relating to the acquisition and maintenance of premises

12.7.1.3 Further Education

1. Teacher Training Colleges: Building Grant Files 1904-1924 (ED 87)
    - acquisition, erection and improvement of premises

2. Further Education: National Colleges 1944-1970 (ED 165)
    - schemes for the establishment of colleges

3. Further Education: Major Establishments 1923-1979 (ED 168)
    - approval of institutions, title, buildings and property

12.7.2 Endowment Files

1. Elementary Education: Endowment Files 1853-1945 (ED 49)
    - administration of endowments; schemes and orders

2. Secondary Education: Endowment Estate Management Files 1894-1924 (ED 43)
    - management of estates, property and other assets

12.7.3 Local Authority Files

1. School Districts 1848-1910 (MH 27)
    - accommodation, staffing, building loans; auditors' statements; inspectors' reports; London school board expenditure

2. Nursery Education: Local Education Authority Files 1918-1966 (ED 66)
    - proposals for nursery schools and classes; reports on areas; 1936 survey

3. School Board Office and Pupil Teacher Centre Files 1884-1911 (ED 57)
    - papers relating to the establishment of such offices and centres, acquisition of sites and premises, alterations to premises, loans for such purposes, and the sale of sites and premises

4. 1944 Education Act: Primary and Secondary Schools Development Plans 1945-1966 (ED 152)
    - plans for special schools; protests; and relevant supply papers

5. Local Education Authority Major Building Projects: Registered Files 1946-1976 (ED 154)
    - concerning the extension of existing accommodation, the building of new schools and the supply of additional places after the school leaving age was raised in 1947

12.7.4   General Policy Files

1.   Committee of the Privy Council on Education, Minutes and Reports 1839-
      1899 (ED 17)
      -      information on the denomination, month of inspection, annual and
             building grants, attendance and from 1878 accommodation of each
             school

2.   Private Office Papers 1851-1935 (ED 24)
      -      surviving records of the Private Office and some papers of Sir
             William Anson relating to his term of office as Parliamentary
             Secretary to the Board of Education, 1902-1905

3.   Inspectorate Memoranda 1878-1941 (ED 22)
      -      copies of circulars and memoranda issued to HMIs

4.   Science and Art Department Building Grants 1860-1904 (ED 29)
      -      applications from trustees of science and art schools for building
             grants, details of grants made and applications refused

5.   General Education, General Files 1865-1945 (ED 10)
      -      general files concerned with the administration of the Education Acts

6.   Private Office: Files and Papers 1935-1966 (ED 136)
      -      similar to ED 24; committee papers, working papers

7.   Circulars and Administrative Memoranda 1870-1989 (ED 142)
      -      official communications issued by the Department to local education
             authorities and other educational establishments

8.   Establishment Files 1835-1971 (ED 23)
      -      includes files relating to the Architects and Building Branch

9.   Architects and Building Branch: Registered Files 1936-1969 (ED 150)
      -      documents relating to the development progress and policy of
             building of educational premises since the Second World War

10.   Architects and Building Branch: Registered Files (A & B series) 1958-1970
      (ED 203)
      -      provision of school buildings, the effects of raising the school leaving
             age and the introduction of the metric system for buildings

11.   Architects and Building Branch Publications 1968-1986 (ED 173)
      -      technical publications issued by the branch and relating to the design
             and building of educational premises

12. Chief Architects of Consortia Committee: Minutes and Papers 1967-1971 (ED 199)
     -     minutes and papers of the CAOC of the educational building consortia of local authorities

13. Further Education: Building Programme: Files 1936-1966 (ED 160)
     -     consultations and proposals; materials concerned; loan sanctions; and details of land of Housing and Local Government

14. University Grants Committee: Registered Files 1909-1988 (UGC 7)
     -     registered files covering all aspects of the work of the Committee

Figure 21
Specimens of official Ministry of Education seals and stamps, 1936-1944 (ED 23/802)

SELECT BIBLIOGRAPHY
AND FURTHER READING

Argles, M, *South Kensington to Robbins* (Longmans, 1964)

Association of Teachers of Domestic Science, *A Survey of the Teaching of Domestic Science in Secondary Schools* (Campfield Press, St Albans, 1968)

Ball, N, *Her Majesty's Inspectorate 1839-1849* (Oliver and Boyd, Edinburgh, 1963)

Barnard, H C, *A History of English Education* (University of London Press, 1969)

Baylis, R, 'Home Economics and the Special Reports', *Journal of Educational Administration and History*, vol vii no 1 (1975), pp 18-27

Bidder, M G and Baddeley, F, *Domestic Economy in Theory and Practice* (CUP, 1901)

Bishop, A S, 'Ralph Lingen, Secretary to the Education Department 1849-1870', *British Journal of Educational Studies*, vol xxi no 2 (June 1968), pp 138-163

Clarke, L, *The Inspector Remembers. Diary of One of Her Majesty's Inspectors of Schools 1936-1970* (Dennis Dobson, 1976)

Clay, F, *Modern School Buildings* (Batsford, 1902)

Cook, G and Gosden, P, *Education Committees* (Councils and Education, 1986)

Curtis, S J and Boultwood, M E A, *An Introductory History of English Education since 1800* (University Tutorial Press, Cambridge 1967)

Dent, H C, *The Training of Teachers in England and Wales 1800-1975* (Hodder & Stoughton, 1977)

Department of Education and Science, Her Majesty's Inspectorate of Schools, *1839-1989 Public Education in England 150th Anniversary* (HMSO, 1990)

Fairbairn, A N, *The Leicestershire Plan* (Heinemann, 1980)

Fletcher, S, *Feminists and Bureaucrats. A study in the development of girls' education in the nineteenth century* (Cambridge University Press, 1980)

Gamlin, R, *Modern School Hygiene* (Aberdeen University Press, 1954)

Gordon, P, 'Commitments and Developments in the Elementary School Curriculum 1870-1907', *History of Education*, vol 6 no 1 (1977), pp 43-52

Gordon, P, 'The Holmes-Morant Circular of 1911: A Note', *Journal of Educational Administration and History*, vol x no 1 (1978), pp 36-40

Gordon, P, *The Study of the Curriculum* (Batsford, 1981)

Gordon, P and Lawton, D, *Curriculum Change in the nineteenth and twentieth centuries* (Hodder and Stoughton, 1978)

Gordon, P and Lawton, D, *HMI* (Routledge and Kegan Paul, 1987)

Gosden, P H J H, *The Development of Educational Administration in England and Wales* (Blackwell, 1966)

Gosden, P H J H, *Education in the Second World War* (Methuen, 1976)

Gosden, P H J H, *The Education System since 1944* (Martin Robertson, 1983)

History of Education Society, *Studies in the government and control of education since 1860* (Methuen and Co Ltd, 1970)

Jenkins, T R, 'Teacher Training in Welsh Colleges of Education 1960-1970', *Journal of Educational Administration and History*, vol vii no 2 (1975), pp 31-39

Kogan, M and Packwood, T, *Advisory Councils and Committees in Education* (Routledge and Kegan Paul, 1974)

Lawton, D, *The Politics of the School Curriculum* (Routledge and Kegan Paul, 1980)

Maclure, S, *Educational Documents, 1816-1963* (Chapman and Hall, 1965)

Maclure, S, *One Hundred Years of London Education 1870-1970* (Allen Lane, 1970)

Maclure, S, *Educational Development and School Building: Aspects of Public Policy 1945-73* (Longman, 1977)

Plaskow, M (ed), *Life and Death of the Schools Council* (Falmer Press, 1985)

Ravenhill, A, 'Domestic Science and the Domestic Arts', *The Journal of Education* (Nov 1907), pp 775-777

Richmond, W K, *The School Curriculum* (Methuen and Co Ltd, 1971)

Richmond, W K, *Education in Britain since 1944* (Methuen and Co Ltd, Cambridge 1978)

Shorney, D, *Teachers in Training 1906-1985 A History of Avery Hill College* (Thames Polytechnic, 1989)

Sillitoe, H, *A History of the Teaching of Domestic Subjects* (Methuen, 1933)

Simon, B, *Studies in the History of Education, 1780-1870* (Lawrence and Wishart, 1960)

Simon, B, *Education and the Labour Movement, 1870-1920* (Lawrence and Wishart, 1965)

Simon, B, *The Politics of Education Reform, 1920-1940* (Lawrence and Wishart, 1974)

Simon, B, *Education and the Social Order, 1940-1990* (Lawrence and Wishart, 1991)

Sneyd-Kinnersley, E M, *H. M. I. Some Passages in the Life of one of H. M. Inspectors of Schools* (Macmillan, 1910)

Sutherland, G, *Policy-Making in Elementary Education 1870-1895* (OUP, 1973)

Taylor, P W, 'The Development of Higher Technological Education in Britain 1945-1951', *Journal of Educational Administration and History*, vol vii no 2 (1975), pp 20-30

The Architect's Journal, May 28th 1936

Wilkinson, M, 'The Holmes Circular Affair', *Journal of Educational Administration and History*, vol xii no 2 (1980), pp 29-38

INDEX

—, Hadow Report *(Education and the Adolescent)* (1926), 3.11, 3.13, 4.5, 4.6, 4.10.4, 10.3.3, 11.10.1.2
—, Hadow Report, *(The Primary School)*, (1931), 3.11
—, *Half our Future* (Newsom Report) (1963), 4.8
—, Henniker-Heaton Report on day-release, (1964), 5.9.3
—, Lockwood Report on curriculum and examinations, (1963), 11.8
—, McNair Report on the supply, training and recruitment of teachers (1942), 9.10, 9.15, 10.4
—, Newcastle Commission Report on state of popular education, (1861), 1.4, 3.4, 10.2.2, 11.1
—, Newsom Report *(Half our Future)* (1963), 4.8
—, Norwood Report on secondary school curriculum and examinations (1943), 10.4, 11.4, 11.6
—, Oxford and Cambridge Universities (1873), 7.2.2
—, Oxford University (1852), 7.2.1
—, Oxford University (1854-1858), 7.2.1
—, Percy Report on higher technological education, (1945), 5.9.1
—, Plowden Report *(Children and their Primary Schools)* (1967), 3.13
—, Ravenhill Report *(The Teaching of Domestic Science in the USA)*, 11.10.1
—, *Report from the Select Committee on Education and Science* (1967), 10.4
—, *Report of the Commissioners for Taking a census of Great Britain on Education* (1852-1853), 3.4

—, *Report of the Committee of Inquiry into the Education of Handicapped Children and Young People* (Warnock), (1978), 8.2.1
—, *Report of the Committee on the Civil Service* (Fulton Report) (1967-1968), 10.4
—, *Report of the Royal Commission on the Civil Service* (1929-1931), 10.3.1
—, *Report of the Society for the Bettering of the Condition of the Poor,* 3.8
—, *Report on the Organization of the Permanent Civil Service* (Northcote-Trevelyan Report), (1853), 2.2
—, Russell Report *(Adult Education: A Plan for Development)* (1973), 5.9.4
—, Spens Report *(Report of the Consultative Committee of the Board of Education on Secondary Education with Special Reference to Grammar Schools and Technical High Schools)* (1938), 3.13, 4.5, 4.6, 11.2
—, *The Primary School,* (Hadow), (1931), 3.11
—, *The Teaching of Domestic Science in the USA* (Ravenhill Report), 11.10.1.1
—, *The Training of Pauper Children* (1838), 9.3
—, Waddell Report on secondary school examinations and syllabuses, (1977-1978), 11.8
—, Warnock Report, *(Report of the Committee of Inquiry into the Education of Handicapped Children and Young People)* (1978), 8.2.1, 8.2.2
Research and Planning Branch, 5.9.5
'Responsible Bodies', 5.8
Revised Code, 9.3, 10.1.2, 11.1
see also code